Dignity for All

*To my partner, Doug, for all of your support,
encouragement, and guidance.*

Dignity for All

SAFEGUARDING LGBT STUDENTS

PETER DEWITT

A JOINT PUBLICATION

CORWIN
A SAGE Company

NASP

CORWIN
A SAGE Company

FOR INFORMATION

Corwin
A SAGE Company
2455 Teller Road
Thousand Oaks, California 91320
www.corwin.com

SAGE Publications Ltd.
1 Oliver's Yard
55 City Road
London, EC1Y 1SP
United Kingdom

SAGE Publications Pvt. Ltd.
B 1/I 1 Mohan Cooperative Industrial Area
Mathura Road, New Delhi 110 044
India

SAGE Publications Asia-Pacific Pte. Ltd.
3 Church Street
#10-04 Samsung Hub
Singapore 049483

Acquisitions Editor: Arnis Burvikovs
Associate Editor: Desirée A. Bartlett
Editorial Assistant: Kimberly Greenberg
Project Editor: Veronica Stapleton
Copy Editor: Amy Rosenstein
Typesetter: Hurix Systems Pvt. Ltd
Proofreader: Dennis W. Webb
Indexer: Molly Hall
Cover Designer: Michael Dubowe
Permissions Editor: Karen Ehrmann

Printed in the United States of America

Library of Congress Cataloging-in-Publication Data

DeWitt, Peter.

  Dignity for all : safeguarding LGBT students / Peter DeWitt.

  p. cm.

  A joint publication with the National Association of School Psychologists.

  Includes bibliographical references and index.

  ISBN 978-1-4522-0590-8 (pbk.)

  1. Homosexuality and education–United States. 2. Lesbian students–United States. 3. Gay students–United States. 4. Bisexual students–United States. 5. Transgender youth–Education–United States. 6. Schools–Safety measures–United States–Handbooks, manuals, etc. I. Title.

  LC192.6.D48 2012

  371.826'64–dc23

                                    2011049859

This book is printed on acid-free paper.

12 13 14 15 16 10 9 8 7 6 5 4 3 2 1

Contents

Preface

PURPOSE

Lesbian, gay, bisexual, and transgender (LGBT) youth are coming out at an earlier age than they did in years past. Many young adults in the LGBT community come out by the age of 15, and some have known their sexual identity since the age of 10. LGBT students who identify as lesbian, gay, bisexual, and transgender often fear the consequences of coming out at such a young age. They fear losing friends and family and are often threatened by their peers. LGBT students are more likely to be harassed or abused by peers, which can negatively affect their school engagement and performance.

In order for students to be engaged in school, they must feel safe in their school environment. School personnel can help this often mistreated group by providing safeguards and supports to protect LGBT students. School administrators have the influence and duty to create those safeguards and supports, and therefore, can have a profound impact on LGBT students. Safeguards and supports include codes of conduct and board policies as well as offering curriculum, resources, and after-school opportunities. This book explores safeguards and supports to help engage LGBT students.

WHO SHOULD READ THIS BOOK

Educators who believe they can change their school culture will gain insight by reading *Dignity for All: Safeguarding LGBT Students* because there are personal stories from the field as well as practical tips on how they can safeguard and support LGBT students in schools.

Creating safe spaces, incorporating curriculum, and establishing Gay–Straight Alliances (GSA) are some of the ways educators can help LGBT students. Action steps are provided in this book to help educators find ways to make LGBT students feel safer in school. In addition, establishing a more accepting school climate will help students who come from diverse backgrounds feel more welcome in schools.

Administrators need to read this book. As a practicing administrator, I understand that I influence the culture of the building, and teachers will only feel that they can step out of their comfort zone if I provide them with the environment to do so. It is an administrator's job to make staff and students feel safe so that students can explore a diverse curriculum that will help them become career and college ready. In addition, I understand that we need safeguards in our code of conduct as well as our school board policies so that we have support as we confront issues with parents and students. I have tried my best to provide steps to bring administrators closer to those safeguards in their school system. When all is said and done, every single student who enters school doors deserves an education that will help foster their imagination and help them find their strengths. It should not matter what their race, gender, religion, or sexual orientation is, and it is not the job of educators to be the gatekeepers to a quality education. All students deserve it.

In addition, this is an important resource for parents. Parents have a role in the education of their children and deserve a place in the discussions that affect their children every day. When we involve parents in the discussions about our school systems, we get another voice that can lead to a stronger, more inclusive school system. The reality is that there are parents who disown their children when they identify as LGBT. This sad reality can happen for numerous reasons, but one of the biggest is that parents have not been exposed to people in the LGBT community. This book will offer resources to parents who lack exposure to LGBT issues.

THE GOAL OF THIS BOOK

Through stories from LGBT students and adults, readers will be exposed to the real-life experiences of these individuals. This book will encourage educators to make at least one change in their classrooms or schools that will help an LGBT student feel safer and more welcome. A friend told me that he saw an LGBT student from Rochester, New York, speak once, and the teenager stood up in front of a crowd of educators and said, "You don't have to do everything; you just have to do something." It is not my intention for readers to think they have to make every change I suggest, although that would be great, too. It is my intention to offer suggestions on where educators can make changes, and have them make one or two changes in their classrooms or schools. That alone may help an insecure LGBT student feel more secure.

Changing a school system to be more inclusive for LGBT students is a net positive for all students because it provides them with the exposure to diverse people, which will help them when they reach adulthood and enter society. If it is good enough for a heterosexual student, it should be good enough for an LGBT student as well.

THE APPROACH OF THIS BOOK

I am a former elementary school teacher and a practicing elementary school principal. I work with students at their level, which means I do not use a great deal of educational jargon and try not to use big words. Although some readers may be uncomfortable addressing this issue, the book is designed to be a reader-friendly resource. I have included current and past research on all issues regarding LGBT students. I begin with why this is a timely and worthwhile topic, and then the book explores bullying, curriculum, GSAs, and school board policies, all of which will create a more inclusive school. Although the book does focus on the bullying of LGBT students, the suggestions I make can help with all bullying, not just one minority group.

Readers should use this as both a handbook and a resource for a book-club discussion. I believe debate can be a healthy and enriching experience, and this book will inspire debates among readers. I understand that not everyone approves of homosexuality and many do not wish to highlight it in any way. That can have many negative effects on all students. Although not many people enjoy confrontation, it can be constructive when it leads to a better place among educators.

Every chapter has both action steps and discussion questions. Action steps will provide readers with guidance when exploring adding safeguards to board policies and codes of conduct. The action steps will also help guide readers who want to begin a GSA in their school as well as providing guidance to those who wish to develop parent outreach programs. In addition to the action steps are discussion questions that readers can use for book-club discussions. Those questions can also be used if you are reading this book solely to find useful information. They may help you process each chapter after you read it.

WHY READERS SHOULD BUY THIS BOOK

I do not expect all readers to agree with my opinions, advice, and guidance. To some this book may offer good suggestions that they can use in their school. As an openly gay administrator, I understand that this book may be very controversial, and readers will struggle with some of my suggestions. It all depends where readers live and what they have been exposed to in their lives. Regardless of their circumstances, readers will gain insight into LGBT student and parent populations that they will come into contact with, and they deserve to be treated with the same level of respect as their heterosexual peers.

Second, this book acts as a resource for educators when they begin to implement changes in their classrooms and schools. They need to know what to be aware of and have insight into how some community members and colleagues will react when they broach the topic of safeguarding LGBT students. I believe this book will be that resource to educators in a respectful way. It is not my intention to preach to readers why this is important; it is my intention to motivate others to start thinking about why this topic needs to be addressed.

Third, regardless of what readers do with this book after they finish it, they will have a better understanding of how to change the school culture in their buildings. After reading this book, teachers can help change their classroom culture, which will begin a grassroots effort to change the culture in their schools. For administrators, this book will put a minority group of students on the radar, and by making simple changes to language, what is hung up on school walls, what appears on the school website, and what groups are allowed in the school, administrators will change the building's culture for the better, which will have a direct impact on all students.

Acknowledgments

I would like to thank the following people who have helped my career in many different ways.

Michelle Hebert, my editor and friend from SAANYS. Thank you for believing in my voice.

Isabel Lim, Kathy Barrans, and Elaine Houston from WNYT (Albany, NBC affiliate).

My *Education Week* editors, Stacy Morford and Elizabeth Rich.

Ray O'Connell, Ann Myers, Jim Butterworth, Lee Wilson, Mark Stratton, Lori Caplan, and Maureen Long from the SAGE College Doctoral Program.

Joe Kosciw, Eliza Byard, Daryl Presgraves, and Robert McGarry from GLSEN for their information, countless conversations, and friendship.

Diane Ravitch for helping me find the courage to speak up.

Arnis Burvikovs and Desirée A. Bartlett for the opportunity to publish with Corwin. It has been an honor to work with both of you.

Thank you to my administrative colleagues, staff, and students for all of your support over the years (Saint Gregory's, Arlington, Glens Falls, Watervliet, and Averill Park).

Most importantly, I would like to thank my mom, siblings, family, and friends for their support and encouragement over the years.

Thanks Dad. You've always been here.

Publisher's Acknowledgments

Corwin would like to thank the following individuals for taking the time to provide their editorial insight and guidance:

Marie Blum, Superintendent
Canaseraga Central School District
Canaseraga, New York

Dalane E. Bouillion, Associate Superintendent
    for Curriculum & Instructional Services
Spring Independent School District
Houston, Texas

Connie C. Hanel, Corwin Author
Academic Achievement Specialist
Medaille College
Buffalo, New York

Kathleen Hwang, Principal
Sanders Corner Elementary School
Ashburn, Virginia

Susan Kessler, Executive Principal
Hunters Lane High School
Nashville, Tennessee

Amanda S. Mayeaux, Master Teacher
Glen Oaks Middle School
Baton Rouge, Louisiana

Michael McMann, Director of Climate and Culture
Fort Vermilion School Division
Fort Vermilion, Alberta, Canada

Diane Smith, School Counselor
Smethport Area High School
Smethport, Pennsylvania

About the Author

 **Peter DeWitt, EdD,** has been a principal in upstate New York since 2006. Prior to being a principal, he taught elementary school in several city schools for 11 years. In addition, Peter is an adjunct professor in the Graduate School of Education at the College of Saint Rose and has presented at state and national conferences around the United States.

Since July 2011, Peter has been writing a blog titled "Finding Common Ground," which is published by *Education Week.* In addition, he is a freelance writer for *Vanguard* magazine (School Administrators Association of New York State) and the International Center for Leadership in Education (ICLE). His articles have appeared in education journals at the state, national, and international levels.

CHAPTER ONE

The Silent Minority

Things will get better. And more than that, with time you're going to see that your differences are a source of pride and a source of strength. You'll look back on the struggles you've faced with compassion and wisdom. And that's not just going to serve you, but it will help you get involved and make this country a better place.
—President Barack Obama (Savage & Miller, 2011, p. 9)

OUR SCHOOL EXPERIENCES

Some students in our public school system fit into the school culture without an issue. Many of these students go through their school experience unscathed because they are popular, good looking, or a good athlete, or they do well in school. They enter school each day feeling engaged and safe, and when they get older, as we all do, they will probably remember their high school days as one of the best times of their lives.

These students grow up, attend college, or go into the workforce and most likely do well, just like they did in high school. They attend their 10th, 20th, and 25th high school reunions where they talk about the "good ole days" when they scored the winning touchdown or pulled a great class prank, kissed their first girl, or had their first beer. When meeting up with old friends, they see their high school experience as the solid foundation to whom they became as an adult.

We have another segment of our K–12 students who feel differently. They do not fit in, were never popular, no one gives them a second glance, unless of course it is to abuse them for being different. Many of these students do not go a day unscathed and are more

1

likely to never attend a high school reunion or remember school fondly. They cannot wait to graduate and get out, and typically vow to never return to their roots because they were gay and their peers knew it. Their memories often include being called a "faggot," "homo," or "dyke."

The unfortunate fact is, according to the Gay, Lesbian, Straight Education Network (GLSEN) *2009 National School Climate Survey*, "84.6% of LGBT students reported being verbally harassed, 40.1% reported being physically harassed and 18.8% reported being physically assaulted at school in the past year because of their sexual orientation." In addition, "72.4% heard homophobic remarks, such as 'faggot' or 'dyke,' frequently or often at school" (2009, p. 26).

With any luck, lesbian, gay, bisexual, and transgender (LGBT) students attend a college where they meet other "like-minded" people, find their niche, and become successful. Unfortunately, that may not be the norm for many of our students, and as early as elementary school we recognize who some of those students will be, and we do not always do enough about it.

> "Growing up is, for all children, a process of discovering who they are in relation to self and others. In a predominately heterosexual society constantly and pervasively reinforcing heterosexual behavior, identity conflict will inevitably occur for most persons who have a homosexual orientation." (Marinoble, 1998, p. 54)

Parents play an important role in the growth and development of students. However, sometimes we underestimate the role that we as educators play in their development. Either that, or we just choose not to recognize it so we feel better about the fact that these students are not fitting in. As educators, we find ourselves saying, "Yeah, kids can be tough on one another," or "I just wish he would act differently so he doesn't make himself a target."

What if we could do things differently? What if we could make an impact on these students? What if we found ways to engage them through curriculum or after-school activities, or made them feel welcome in our schools by providing a safe space? Many LGBT students feel threatened, unloved, and alone. Sure, there are those LGBT students who are fortunate enough to grow up in a supportive household where they are loved. They go to a supportive high school that educates the whole child and creates diverse experiences for them, which will help them grow into contributing members of society. However, I would venture to guess that is not the norm.

"Whether manifested or not, there is a sense of being somehow different than the world expects them to be, and this is a source of considerable identity conflict for most homosexual students" (Marinoble, 1998, p. 55).

Over the past few years, there has been a slew of suicides. The young people who have died by suicide range from kids who did not reach the teenage years to others who cut their lives short before they finished college. It is clear that we have an issue in our society that needs to be changed, and those of us who are fortunate enough to call education our choice of career can help change it.

As an elementary school principal, I have seen children walk through our halls being able to be who they are, and having teachers and other students support them in their endeavors, such as wearing outrageous clothing or flirting with gender norms by wearing their hair short if they are a girl or long if they are a boy. I had a male student who liked to wear a long scarf and say that he wanted to grow up and be a female supermodel. He did not do it to make fun of anyone; he did it because that is how he felt. Kids with individuality should be encouraged and applauded rather than forced to change and fit in. Every student should have the same opportunities, no matter their race, gender, religion, or sexual orientation.

However, the harsh reality is that I do not see all the teasing and torment that goes on in our school, and I think we can change that. Our LGBT student population is the most marginalized. Every time we turn the other cheek, we have lost another student and helped prevent them from finding themselves. When we ignore opportunities to help those students, we give them a reason to hate the school system.

Teenage years are hard enough because of all the storm and stress that happens with our studies, family relationships, and friends. Having the extra element of needing to hide who you are because others will not like or love you anymore, including your family, is painful. LGBT students painfully walk in our doors everyday trying to be someone they are not, and our society does not make that any easier.

Our LGBT students are dropping out of school at an alarming rate. They experiment with drugs and alcohol at a higher rate than their straight peers, and are more likely to suffer from depression.

According to Thiede and colleagues, "[Sixty-six percent] reported use of illicit drugs; 28%, use of 3 or more drugs; 29%, frequent drug use (once a week or more); and 4%, injection drug use" (2003, p. 1915). "For heterosexual students, alcohol is the most commonly used drug among high school students with 35.4% of 10th- and 48.6% of 12th-grade students reported to have used it" (Burrow-Sanchez & Lopez, 2009, p. 72). A supportive school environment may not change that abuse of alcohol and drugs, but it can go a long way in helping these students find their niche in life.

WHAT IT MEANS TO BE GAY

"I knew I was gay when the most exciting part of my Bar Mitzvah was meeting the party planner" (Trachtenberg & Bachtell, 2005, p. 5).

Members of the LGBT community will tell you they knew they were gay at a very young age. In the decades leading up to the new millennium, people in the LGBT community did not feel as if they could be openly gay in society, let alone within their own communities. Many went on to get married only to come out at a later age, after they had children and found that they could no longer hide who they are. A large percentage of gay and lesbian women did not come out in high school because they feared the chance that they would be disowned by loved ones. Many of them did not even realize they were gay because they lacked role models in the LGBT community and were never exposed to gay characters on television or in books.

Identifying, whether privately or publicly, as gay or lesbian can be a very traumatic experience for anyone, regardless of their age, income level, or the level of support they get from their family. It can be especially difficult for a teenager who has to enter a school setting on a daily basis. Sears states, "Our capacity to relate emotionally and physically to other human beings is not limited to the other gender" (1991, p. 54). LGBT youth are coming out at an earlier age, with some coming out as young as 12 years old (Horowitz & Itzkowitz, 2011). Many young adults in the LGBT community come out by the age of 15, and some have known their sexual identity since the age of 10 (Ryan, 2009, p. 1).

There are a variety of steps those going through the experience can take after this realization. One possible step is to hide those feelings and try to fit in with their heterosexual peers, which has often been done in the school setting. Another step is to "come out" to friends and family by openly admitting to being LGBT. This act of coming out often takes a great deal of thought and reflection because there is a possibility that the teenager coming out could lose close friends or be disowned by family. Fearing the loss of being disowned by those you love because you have feelings for someone of the same sex is a terrifying experience.

Harbeck states, "Many of us have grown up with a feeling that our being lesbian, gay or bisexual (LGB) is bad, and that we must hide it" (1995, p. 126). Being openly gay is not easy for many students and adults. Society is predominantly straight, and the word gay is constantly used in a derogatory manner. LGBT people know they are different, and they are often reminded of that fact on a daily basis. It takes time, reflection, and strength to overcome those realities. Over the past year, there have been countless stories about youths who died by suicide because they were perceived to be gay.

> What can clearly be referred to as a continuing epidemic, within only the past few weeks, a number of gay young men have taken their lives by all indications as a result of the unrelenting homophobic taunts, harassment, and attacks they had to endure by their peers: Seth Walsh, 13, hung himself from a tree outside his California home; Billy Lucas, 15, hung himself in Indiana; Asher Brown, 13, from Texas, shot himself in the head; Tyler Clementi, 18, a first-year student from Rutgers University, took his life by jumping off the George Washington Bridge. (Blumenfeld, 2010, para. 1)

This sad slew of suicides that has taken our young people has taught us that we have an epidemic involving LGBT teens and that we need to do our best to make it stop. Our schools are the places where we can teach students about acceptance and also teach students how to accept who they are.

Whether LGBT students are out or "in the closet," there is a feeling of guilt. These individuals long to be accepted, and they are at risk of looking anywhere to find that acceptance. If they are in the closet, there are a variety of mixed emotions. Closeted LGBT students feel guilty for not being honest to their families, friends, and themselves. In addition, they feel ashamed for the feelings they have. Not having anyone to turn to for guidance and support can be debilitating and a very lonely experience. That feeling of aloneness is why LGBT students make unsafe decisions.

THE NEED FOR ROLE MODELS

> "During my childhood and young adulthood, gays and lesbians were invisible in my community. But while they were invisible, they certainly were not absent; their presence was just not acknowledged. The behaviors I observed in the adults I loved and looked up to suggested that gays and lesbians were people one whispered about; spoke of in vague, masked terms; or ridiculed, abused, and violated because of who and what they were. The world that formed me and shaped my values did not honor, afford humanity to, or bestow dignity on those who were gay. I grew up in a world where gay, lesbian, and bisexual people were invisible, isolated, powerless, and voiceless" (Roper, 2005, p. 81).

As much as society has changed, same-sex couples can still not get married in well over 40 states, and they do not have the same rights as their heterosexual friends and family—LGBT teens who have not come out yet know that fact. They watch television and hear negative conversations about the LGBT community. In the 2012 presidential campaign, Michele Bachmann was accused of calling LGBT people "barbarians," and her husband was accused of offering reparative therapy to gays and lesbians in an effort to change them to become heterosexual (Ross, Schwartz, Mosk, & Chuchmach, 2011). "She once likened it to personal bondage, personal despair and personal enslavement" (Stolberg, 2011, p. 1).

Worse than that, closeted LGBT students could potentially hear the opinions that their loved ones feel about gay people. Unlike other minorities, being in the closet provides you with insight into two worlds. One world is the life you know, surrounded by family and friends. However, those family and friends, not knowing they have a gay member of their own family, could potentially talk about their dislike for members of the LGBT community. Even before a student may know they are gay, she is hit by many images that offer an anti-gay sentiment on television or through conversations at home if she lives within a conservative household. That sends a very powerful message to our LGBT youth.

"Most adolescents realize that the expression of homosexual feelings within the dominant peer group, where there is tremendous pressure to conform to heterosexual norms, will result in alienation from peers at best, and violence at worst" (Anderson, 1995, p. 24). All students face those heterosexual norms in the public school setting, where students often feel stress about fitting in with their peers.

The other world, the one the LGBT students want to belong to, is the group of their LGBT peers, where they can find like-minded friends and perhaps even a partner. Teens in the LGBT community lack role models around them and are typically in the minority with their peers. Anderson says, "It is not surprising that gay and lesbian adolescents, wanting involvement in a peer group that accepts them, and offers the possibility of establishing intimate relationships, often begin to search for other gay persons" (1995, p. 25). Most heterosexual teens can look to their parents or other members of society to learn about gender roles in relationships, but LGBT teens often cannot do the same. LGBT teens do not always have positive gay role models in their lives and often have to identify with what they see on television.

Books, films, classroom discussions, guest speakers, and field trips almost always reinforce heterosexual norms and values. Lesbian and gay adults, teachers and other school staff, most often are closeted, depriving gay and lesbian youth of positive role models. (Marinoble, 1998, p. 55)

HARASSMENT AND DISCRIMINATION OF LGBT STUDENTS

While the intersections of social class, race, gender, sexuality, and religion vary for each person, their existence and importance within our culture are, for those who do not share membership in the dominant groups, social facts with social consequences. (Sears, 1991, p. 55)

At a time in life when teenagers do not want to be seen as different from their peers, being gay, which puts students in the minority of a school population, makes those students feel as if a spotlight is on them and often opens them up to harassment and verbal abuse. That type of discrimination creates a fear for students as they walk into the public school setting. These students who have "come out" as gay or lesbian often hear harassing remarks from peers, and other students who are gay and lesbian do not come out at all in fear that they will lose friends and alienate themselves from their families. This discrimination that sexually diverse students face creates a feeling of helplessness and isolation, which leads some students in the LGBT community to drop out of school or run away from home.

Unks explains, "Picking on persons because of their ethnicity, class, religion, gender, or race is essentially taboo behavior, but adults and children alike are given license to torment and harm because of their sexuality" (1995, p. 3). Although that quotation is from the mid-1990s, it still holds true today because LGBT students are being bullied and harassed frequently. This fear of torment, discrimination, and the isolation gay and lesbian teenagers face when coming out can be detrimental to their existence, not only as students in a school system, but as human beings as well. The constant concern about losing those around you is a debilitating experience. Having the right support system, whether it is through school, friendships, or family, is vitally important:

> No one should underestimate the value of teachers' including gay people when they talk with students about cultural diversity. Just hearing the words "homosexuality" or "gay/lesbian/ bisexual" in an accepting context sends a powerful message to young people, and creates the potential for a tolerant environment. (Lipkin, 1995, p. 39)

GLSEN is doing landmark research in the area of sexual diversity and school climate. GLSEN's 2005 report stated the following:

> As leaders of their schools, principals strive to ensure a positive learning environment for all students; one where students feel safe and free from harassment. Yet for many students who identify as lesbian, gay, bisexual or transgender (LGBT), school can often be a very dangerous place. The 2005 report, *From Teasing to Torment: School Climate in America* by Harris Interactive and GLSEN found that the most common reasons for bullying and harassment in America's middle and high schools were physical appearance, sexual orientation and gender expression,

showing that LGBT-related characteristics account for two of the top three reasons students are singled out for mistreatment. (Kosciw, 2007)

Students who identify as gay and lesbian often face a great deal of criticism and harassment from peers. If this is mixed with a lack of support from home, many gay students turn toward behaviors that can be harmful to them. "One in three has reported committing at least one self-destructive act. Gay and lesbian youth make up approximately one quarter of all homeless youth in the U.S." (Gibson cited in O'Conor, 1995, p. 13). These statistics are staggering, but only through education and awareness can teachers and administrators understand how to meet the needs of these students. Lugg and Shoho (2006) state, "Educators should ensure that public schools would become models of democratic and socially just practices. Quite simply, public schools would become exemplars of American democracy" (p. 200).

NEGATIVE STEREOTYPES OF LGBT STUDENTS

Much of the research in the social justice field revolves around gender, race, and economic status. Sexual orientation is a topic that has been explored, but it is an area that needs further exploration because it affects a large population of students and adults. "The Williams Institute at the UCLA School of Law, a sexual orientation law and public policy think tank, estimates that there are 8.8 million gay, lesbian, and bisexual persons in the U.S based on the 2005/2006 American Community Survey, an extension of the U.S. Census" (Gates, 2006, p. 1).

Most of the existing research revolves around promiscuity, HIV/AIDS, and suicide and mental health services, which are all very grim, but they are realities in the homosexual community. Harbeck states, "With this extreme and sole focus on teen suicide, we may be trading one negative stereotype for another" (1995, p. 126). Although the suicide rate of gay and lesbian teens is high, it is one more perceived negative consequence of being gay to those sexually diverse students who want to come out. Harbeck goes on to say, "Young people who are exploring identities may conclude that suicide is the consequence of being LGBT" (1995, p. 126). We, as educators, need to provide LGBT students with better examples of who they can be and show them that their lives do not have to have a tragic ending.

CONCLUSION

Young gay people come out at different times following their self-awareness and self-identity. In some cases, the person is outed, meaning that their sexual orientation, or perceived sexual orientation, is disclosed by someone else (McNinch & Cronin, 2004, p. 35).

Clearly, LGBT students have a great deal of negative issues facing them as they grow up and mature. Whether they are gay, or perceived as gay, they face the fear of being tormented, which comes in the forms of name calling, physical and psychological punishment, or being outed. Schools can step in and be the positive resource and influence these students need in order to move forward in their lives and help the student become a contributing member of society. In order to properly assist these students, we need to know what issues they face so we can assist them in overcoming those issues. We need to offer supports such as curriculum, student codes of conduct, board policies, and teacher professional development on how to address LGBT issues to allow the students to take ownership over their lives and become successful.

This fragile student population needs support from teachers and administrators because of the discrimination they often feel when they are coming out to peers and family. LGBT students who are supported by teachers and administration feel a sense of safety in their school environment, and that sense of safety allows them to take healthy and positive risks, which builds their engagement in the school community. Students who are engaged in school are more inclined to succeed academically.

Action Steps

- Begin by using the proper language. It is a sexual orientation, not a sexual preference. Preference indicates that they have a choice whether they want to be straight or gay.
- People do not want to be defined by their sexual orientation, but it should not be ignored either. Ask an LGBT student how things are going in school and at home. Reach out in an authentic way.

- If you have openly gay students in your school, ask them if they feel safe. Involve them in the conversation about LGBT safeguards.
- Talk with your school counseling team to see what resources they can offer to LGBT students and their families. Make sure resources such as pamphlets are easily accessible.
- Reading this book shows you care. The best quotation I have heard was from a Rochester, New York, LGBT student who said, "You don't have to do everything. You just have to do something."

Discussion Questions

- Why do you believe some adolescents do not know they are gay until they reach their 20s or attend college?
- Do you know anyone who is LGBT? Have a discussion with your group about someone in the LGBT community that you respect.
- Why do some families disown their LGBT children rather than accept them?
- Why do you feel LGBT students are at risk to experiment with drugs and alcohol?
- Why is it important to reach out to an LGBT student?
- What is one thing you can do to reach out to an LGBT student?

CHAPTER TWO

Bullying of LGBT Students

K eeping classrooms and hallways free of homophobic, sexist, and other types of biased language is a crucial aspect of creating a safe school climate for students. Yet 9 out of 10 students heard these types of biased language in their schools, most commonly anti-LGBT remarks (Gay, Lesbian and Straight Education Network [GLSEN], 2007, p. 4).

As educators, we are bombarded, for what seems like every hour on the hour, with the word "bullying," whether it is from our colleagues, students, parents, or the media. We hear stories about students who are unfairly targeted because of their size, the way they talk, or the way they act. It does not matter if it is a one-time issue or an ongoing issue that has been happening for weeks, months, or years—we hear many adults and children using the word bullying. Unfortunately, most of the bullying issues that we need to address are not bullying at all. They are usually one-time issues between friends who have a misunderstanding. Most students who are being bullied never say anything at all. They are scared that an adult will never address the issue and worry that the bullying will only get worse after they speak out. That fear of retribution is paralyzing.

Perhaps the overuse and misuse of the word bullying happens because we are inundated with 24/7 media, but it is also because there are new tools that the bullies can use to taunt their victims around the clock. One of the most bullied group of students in our public school system come from the lesbian, gay, bisexual, and transgender (LGBT) community.

Today's youths are expressing their sexual identity at younger ages, and this self-awareness is bumping up against the pressure among early adolescents to conform to gender and sexuality norms. Attitudes about same-sex sexuality remain less favorable among early adolescents, yet tend to become more favorable as youths mature. (Russell, 2011, p. 25)

Contrary to popular belief, being picked on does not build character, and it is not a case of a student that needs to get tougher and stop being so sensitive. It will, however, multiply if we do not do anything about it. Bullying is not a discipline issue; bullying is a climate issue, which means we cannot deal with a situation once and expect it to go away. We must create a culture of respect in order to see a decrease in bullying.

As educators, if we want to make a positive impact on all of our students, we need to make sure they all feel safe. If we want our students to be engaged in the educational process, then we must create a safe and nurturing environment that will foster their commitment to school.

Schools have a legal, ethical, and moral obligation to provide equal access to education and equal protection under the law for all students. For many sexual minority students, however, schools are unsafe and survival, not education, is the priority. (Weiler, 2003, p. 10)

In a Utopian environment, or what GLSEN (2010) calls an Inclusive School, our K–12 students would be allowed to follow their own paths and feel they can be their own person without the threat of harassment and physical abuse. However, we know that is not true, and those students who do not fit into societal norms are the ones at risk of being bullied and harassed at school. Our students, no matter what their interests are, should be able to walk in our doors every day and find activities that will help them flourish and be around friends that help nourish their souls. The threat of bullying is a constant worry for students, which can negatively impact their instructional day; bullying happens across North America, which means we have a percentage of students who are only learning how to hate school instead of learning how to prepare for their future.

School is a place where students have the freedom to explore a diverse set of topics, find strengths, and work on weaknesses, all in pursuit of being career and college ready by the time they leave high school. Schools are a microcosm of society at large where they can learn from, and about, people with diverse backgrounds. Bullying can prevent all of that from happening because it makes students want to stay "under the radar" so they are not at risk of being tormented when they walk down the hallways to class. We all know from our varied experiences how mean students can be to one another.

WHERE BULLYING BEHAVIOR BEGINS

Sadly, bullying begins in elementary school, and it often happens during our unstructured times like lunch, recess, and the bus ride to school or home. Bullying has infiltrated all three levels of the public school system from elementary to middle to high school in the 21st century. It rarely happened as early as elementary school. Bullying, much like other risky behavior, has gotten worse. As the students get older, the opportunities for bullying become larger because there is more independent time where students can be cornered by their peers that bully them. Bullying is much more threatening and frightening than the normal day to day storm and stress kids feel. Bullying is targeted behavior toward one child on the part of one or more other children. Bullying isn't just between kids either. It can be between an adult and child as well as between two adults. The reality is that it will never end because it surfaces everywhere we look including reality television and political campaigns. Children see adults participate in it so they participate in it as well. There are a few different types of bullying, which are all used to harass and torment LGBT students.

CYBERBULLYING

A large majority of LGBT students reported being verbally harassed, physically harassed, and physically assaulted at school (GLSEN, 2009, p. 26). Adults often ignore the use of slurs toward LGBT students because it is easier to ignore it go than it is to address it.

As social rituals begin, students are presumed interested in dating the opposite sex. Students brave enough to express concern about their sexual orientation often encounter homophobic teachers, counselors, or administrators who fail to adequately address the issue or make an appropriate referral. (Marinoble, 1998, p. 55)

With 21st century skills come 21st century methods of bullying and harassing students in the LGBT community (DeWitt, 2011). Blogging, social networking, and the use of e-mail are some of the methods used to torment this marginalized population of students. These tools make it hard for a victim to hide, and they include many bystanders on the side who watch as the bully becomes progressively worse. Bystanders are often afraid that they will be the target if they speak up. One example of cyberbullying is that of 18-year-old Tyler Clementi. Tyler Clementi was a student at Rutgers University who died by suicide when he jumped off of the George Washington Bridge on September 22, 2010, after his sexual encounter with a man in his dorm room was secretly videoed by his college roommate without his knowledge and then video streamed over the Internet (Foderaro, 2010).

This is an extreme and sad end to a life, but we have other students who are on the cusp of making the same decision or other students who could make that decision in the near distant future. In order for schools to help, there must be support by school personnel. If bullying is not going to be permanently distinguished, we must at least teach children the harmful effects that their bullying behavior can have on others as well as teach victims how to become resilient and support them as they try to deal with being bullied.

For school personnel to feel engaged in making students feel safe, they must have the support of their building and district administrators. School personnel are much more likely to support students in the LGBT community if they know they will get support from their administrators. Unfortunately, that support does not always happen, which means that administrators and staff condone the behavior—if staff and administrators are not addressing the negative behavior, then they are allowing it to happen. In fact, studies report that teachers and administrators are less likely to intervene on behalf of LGBT students (GLSEN, 2007).

Some education officials, from classroom teachers all the way up to district-level administrators, have tried to remain neutral to avoid conflict within the school community, but this strategy does not promote a welcoming school environment. (Russell, 2011, p. 25)

SETTING THE TONE IN SCHOOL

LGBT students often face the fear of the consequences for disclosing their sexual orientation because they could lose friends and family, and be treated unfairly by others. It is very difficult for these students to feel engaged in school because they are preoccupied with the harsh reality that they could be disowned from their own family if they come out. "There are more than 2.5 million gay students under the age of 18 in the USA" (Gay Straight Alliance, n.d., p. 1). Friend (1998) noted that "as a microcosm, school culture in the United States reflects the conflicts of the broader society" (p. 137). Students who have deep beliefs that are different than their peers tend to keep them hidden because many are afraid to stand out and be different from others. "The culture of the school mirrors the larger society. Schools socialize boys and girls into their presumed heterosexual destiny" (Sears, 1991, p. 55).

These students are in need of support and resources to help get them through this traumatic period of their lives, which is where schools play an important role. If LGBT students are being bullied, they are less likely to seek out an adult to help them because they do not trust those around them for fear that they will just find another adult to treat them unfairly.

"When the principal sneezes, the whole school catches a cold. This is neither good nor bad; it is just the truth. Our impact is significant; our focus becomes the school's focus" (Whitaker, 2003, p. 30). The significant impact that Whitaker (2003) mentions encompasses a wide array of issues. Bielaczyc states, "Clearly, the tone set by the administrator can have a great effect on the culture and attitude of the school population" (2001, p. 9). The culture and attitude to which Bielaczyc (2001) is referring is one of openness and acceptance toward students, regardless of their race, creed, or sexual orientation.

In my experience as an elementary school principal, I have been fortunate enough to work with strong administrators. One such administrator is a high school principal named Colleen Gomes. She received some negative feedback when her high school announced it was going to participate in the GLSEN's "Day of Silence" and "No Name Calling Week." The following is her response to one parent who thought it was wrong that the school would participate in the event.

Vignette

Mr. & Mrs. XXXXX

The "Day of Silence" is sponsored by the Gay, Lesbian, Straight Education Network. From the organization's website, "'The Day of Silence' is about safer schools, tolerance and positive change. Some organizations misrepresent these facts."

Our own extracurricular club (GSA) is the foundation of creating respect for all humans in this building, regardless of race, religion, economic status, physical characteristics or abilities, interests, or sexual orientation. I am proud of the example they set for all of us. They have been a lead group in this building for seven years to promote respect for everyone. The focus this Friday is indeed to respect all...especially homosexuals. I would encourage you to read the heartbreaking story of Lawrence King, a 15-year-old young man who was shot and killed in school in February because of his sexual orientation.

—Mrs. Gomes

The teachers in the building know that they have the support of their administrator, and they feel as if they can better address LGBT issues because of that administrative support.

Although principals should be sensitive to differing perspectives within their school community, they must provide the leadership to ensure a safe and affirming educational environment for all students. (Weiler, 2003, p. 10)

WAYS TO CREATE AN INCLUSIVE SCHOOL COMMUNITY

- Adopt character education words such as respect, acceptance, and honesty. Do not use the word tolerance. People want to be accepted, not tolerated.
- Participate in antibullying campaigns such as GLSEN's "No Name Calling Week."

- *Send staff research-based articles about bullying.*
- *Send staff research-based articles that address bullying of LGBT students.*
- *If you tell staff that using homophobic language is inappropriate, they will listen.*
- *Train staff to address issues they hear and see in the hallway. They cannot ignore those issues. It is easier for staff members to walk away when they hear homophobic language. Teach them how to address it.*
- *Bullying programs are only as good as the staff that uses them. If you are using an antibullying program, make sure staff are trained in how to use it properly.*
- *Ask openly gay students if they feel safe in your school.*
- *Establish a gay–straight alliance in your school.*
- *Students who are exploring gender roles and sexual orientation need assistance. Talk to their parents, guidance counselors, school psychologists, and the students who are questioning their gender or sexual orientation. Ignoring it will not help them process through it.*
- *Help students find a balance between being different than their peers and being a target to their peers. Having conversations is the best way to address this issue.*
- *Students who are actively seeking attention, whether negative or positive, are crying out for help. Help them figure out what they need. Sometimes being a good listener is all that is required.*

SAFEGUARDING AND SUPPORTING LGBT STUDENTS

Besides bullying, but just as prevalent, is the verbal harassment of LGBT students. Although this is an issue all students face, it is more widespread among sexually diverse students. Students hear homophobic remarks while walking down the hallway to class. It is up to the teachers and staff patrolling the hallways to step in and prevent this from happening. They need to intervene and protect this student population from harmful words and threats. Adults are more likely to intervene if they have received professional development.

Professional development around LGBT issues provides staff with the proper methods of intervention to de-escalate harmful situations. There is a great deal of research that supports this statement. Cha (2003) states, "Previous research has found that leadership attitude (supervisory support or sanction) is the most influential factor in facilitating or hindering trainees' transfer of learning to their workplace" (p. 1). Cha goes on to state

Such concern should promote a belief among team members that the leader will provide them with any support that they might need from him or her. Believing that the leader will provide them with resources and other types of support they need to execute their work successfully should strengthen team members' confidence that they will be successful. (Cha, 2003, p. 1)

These two quotations are very important to the safeguarding of LGBT; educators need to know they are supported because any issues regarding sexual orientation tend to be very controversial. "Despite the greater willingness of some homosexuals to be open about their experiences, many educators continue to avoid the issue of sexual orientation—both in school and with regard to parents—because it is such a volatile social issue" (deMarrais & LeCompte, 1999, p. 321). Offering professional development to staff or curriculum to students involving LGBT issues is also controversial because not all parents and students agree that LGBT issues should be explored in the public school setting. Books that feature LGBT characters are often at risk of being banned. Religion is often a factor in this controversy. The support of a strong school administrator is vitally important.

While the intersections of social class, race, gender, sexuality, and religion vary for each person, their existence and importance within our culture are, for those who do not share membership in the dominant groups, social facts with social consequences. (Sears, 1991, p. 55)

It should be unacceptable that LGBT students come to school afraid of being harmed on a daily basis because of their sexual orientation. Student Codes of Conduct and School Board Policies are important pieces to the conversation about safeguarding sexually diverse students. Without proper policies to support discipline procedures and programs to minimize bullying issues, adults are less likely to hold students accountable for the mistreatment of LGBT students.

The following vignette is not about LGBT bullying, but it highlights a school that is trying to change the climate for all of its students.

Changing the School Climate

Dear Mrs. Penn,

Thank you for the talk that you had with my class and me about Kyle because I have learned that it is not nice {to bully}. I did something this weekend that is community service. We went through our neighborhood and collected money for Japan. We wanted to give it to you.

Love, Michaela (fifth grader)

When I came to Sand Creek Middle School 4 years ago as the Associate Principal, I would never have dreamed that students in our building would develop such empathy for others that they would collect money to help some- one in need over the weekend without any prompting from an adult! Since we began implementing the Olweus Bullying Prevention Program at Sand Creek, members of our school community have taken steps to help others whenever the opportunity has presented itself.

Four short years ago, we did not have a building that fostered empathy among students or adults. No one came to my office excited about a com- munity service project they had undertaken over the weekend. Instead, most of my time was devoted to assigning consequences to students for the hurtful actions and words that they continued to direct toward one another despite my best efforts to end the bullying that I was observing. I was frustrated by the number of students going to our Time Out room because of how poorly they treated one another and found that many members of our staff were equally concerned about the climate of our building. As I continued to reflect on this problem, one sixth grader in particular remained in the forefront of my mind because no matter what consequence she received for her actions, she continued to call others names, put them down, and threaten to fight them if they "gave her attitude." It was when I was having yet another conversa- tion with her about how she treated her peers that I finally asked the correct question and initiated the change that enabled us to get to where we are today. I entered the Time Out room and, after silently reminding myself not to give her yet another lecture about why what she was doing was unacceptable, I instead asked, "Why do you call everyone names and treat them so badly? It really is bullying, and I don't think your actions are showing others the person that you truly are." She slowly turned to me and said, "I'm not a bully. I just don't like how they treat me so what else can I do?"

And so the journey began. That March, classroom teachers, monitors, secretaries, administrators, and parents from throughout our Sand Creek com- munity sat down with Cathy Welling, a certified Olweus trainer, and began to develop a bullying prevention program that would fit the needs of our particular middle school. We learned what bullying is and what bullying is not. We found that most of what we believed to be true about bullies was actually a myth and found that our indirect manner of dealing with bullying behavior was actually perpetuating the very problem we were anxious to solve. The

(Continued)

(Continued)

more we learned about the issue, the more focused we became on our objectives; to send the message that bullying would not be tolerated at Sand Creek Middle School and to rejuvenate the sense of community that had always defined our building. Before we left for the summer, the Bullying Prevention Committee shared what we had learned about bullying with the rest of our staff and began planning how to get the program started in the fall.

As with everything else that we do at Sand Creek Middle School, we went all out with our kick-off event that first September. We called it Creekfest, and the rest, as they say, is history. Something amazing happened that warm September evening when we invited our families, students, and staff to return to the building and come together as a community. Vendors served food, students waited in line to pie the principal and dunk their teachers, and everyone walked around smiling because we could sense that we were on to something. Parents, students, and teachers alike remembered that when we take the time to connect on a more personal level, we all begin to feel better about coming to school whether it be to work, to learn, or to pick up a child at the end of the day. We had found out just how good it would feel to be a part of something bigger than all of us, and no one was willing to let go. That feeling spilled over into our building the next day as students and staff returned to school still smelling of whipped cream from the night before. On that particular day, we were ready to spend time together learning about how to protect our community and enhance the powerful connection we had each felt last evening. As we entered the building that morning, we all received matching T-shirts decorated with the antibullying slogan created by one of our students, providing an outward symbol of our individual commitment to our school. Our day was spent learning about what bullying is and how we were going to work together to empower one another to prevent this divisive behavior from eroding our sense of community. We played some cooperative games and got to know one another as we connected as a building. Before we got on the busses that day, we hugged our building surrounding the bricks and mortar with our hands joined together to show that we care about our school and are united in our efforts to create a community where each and every one of us belong.

Since our first Creekfest event in 2008, we have become more conscious of our efforts to nurture our community and give back to those around us (while having fun at the same time!). In 2009, we set out to break the Guinness World Record for the most people bouncing basketballs at the same time. We might not have broken the record, but we did donate over 1,000 basketballs to local Boys & Girls Clubs of America and supported our districtwide Stuff the Bus campaign as we took turns hopping on our buses and handing the basketballs off to waiting members of the Marine Corps. This year, we felt we were ready to continue our commitment to give back to our community and the world around us throughout the school year instead of solely focusing our efforts on how to get our Sand Creek community off to a good start. Since September of 2010, staff and students at Sand Creek have completed over 20 community service projects (and those are just the ones that we know *about!). As our bullying prevention program has evolved, we at Sand Creek Middle School have found ourselves spending more and more time thinking about how we can, as our slogan this year so aptly states, "Run bullying out of town" by creating a community where it is not accepted. The most powerful change, however, has been observed in the actions of our students and how they respond when bullying takes place.*

During the second year of our program, I received a phone call from a parent that reminded me of the importance of what we have undertaken at Sand Creek. This mother contacted me to report something that had occurred on the bus that afternoon. As the story unfolded, I found myself doubting our program and questioning why we spent so much time talking about bullying only to hear that it was still taking place. Her son had been called names by one of his classmates on the way home that day and was visibly upset as he walked through the door. The amazing thing, however, was how his peers responded making this incident different from those about which I had received calls in the past. As this particular student was being made fun of by one of his sixth-grade peers, another student on the bus stood up and said, "What you are doing is bullying. You are not going to make yourself feel any better by making fun of him. Why don't you just leave him alone? He never did anything to you; he was only being himself." A smile quickly came across my face as I heard the words that this student had spoken. Because we had taken the time to educate our students about what bullying is and the impor-tance of standing up when bullying is taking place, this sixth-grade girl had felt empowered to do something when she was faced with an all too common situation that occurs among school-aged children today.

Have we wiped out bullying at Sand Creek Middle School? Not by a long shot! We have, however, continued to hear stories like the one above about students standing up for one another when bullying is taking place and have found that our students are willing to tell an adult when they are faced with a situation that they know is a form of bullying. If we had not taken the time to educate our students about what bullying is and provided them with the tools to deal with the myriad of experiences that they are faced with when they or their peers are demeaned and humiliated, we would not find that our students were standing up. Instead, we would be just another school where students keep the bullying hidden and adults walk around believing that they don't have a bullying problem. Just like at Sand Creek, the majority of students come to school each and every day ready to learn and excited about being a part of their school community. This majority is just as anxious as we are to create a place where all students feel safe and feel like they belong.

If we as educators take the time to listen to our students, model through our treatment of them and our colleagues just how important relationships are and empower students to act when faced with bullying situations, then we can work with our students to create a learning community where each and every individual who walks through our doors can recognize their potential. As educational leaders, what greater contribution can we make than to empower our students and staff to understand that the ability to affect change is in

(Continued)

(Continued)

each and every one of us? At Sand Creek Middle School, we want our building to be a place where we want to come every day, and we know that we alone have the power to make that happen. Start a chain reaction of kindness in your building; you'll be surprised at just how far it can take you.

—Jill Penn, Associate Principal
Sand Creek Middle School
Colonie, New York

Vignette

Finding Your Voice

Twenty-six years ago I entered public education with passion, idealism, and a belief that my work would have positive impact for students and families. I chose to be a teacher in the field of Special Education partially because I felt my life experience as a Jewish lesbian provided me with a perspective of what it was like to be different from others. I understood what it meant to not always be in the majority and how this is something that students with special needs often experience on a daily basis. For 17 years I taught students at the elementary and secondary level. The days were full of magnificent experiences and filled my soul. I truly felt that my experiences allowed me to reach students and families in an exceptionally meaningful manner. Despite this, never once did the issue of my sexual orientation enter a conversation by either me or others with whom I worked, despite the fact that my partner and I had been together for well over 10 years.

Following these years I moved into administration and held a position as an elementary principal as well as Director of Special Education. I did this for 9 years, able to work with students, staff, and families more extensively than I had done as a teacher. While some close colleagues were aware of my sexual orientation, the vast majority of individuals were unfamiliar with this fact. I struggled to find "my voice" and to integrate my personal and professional life as others were easily able to do. Though the nature of this position made me extremely visible within my district, I swallowed my soul on many occasions. As a long-time political activist surrounded by a large community of family and friends, this contradiction weighed heavily on me.

Over time, this reality has changed. During an extremely difficult time in our district last year where homophobia and hate-filled blogs surfaced, I realized how much this "double-life" was impacting me. My partner and I went on television to show support for gay marriage and this was my first public experience in having a true voice. Since that time, the compartmentalization I had created has gradually diminished. I regret the many years it has taken me to find my voice. I know my silence resulted in distance between students and families over the years. I wonder how this could have been different and how I may have had a stronger impact on others was it not for this issue. Still,

I know the perspective of my life experience was something I carried with me at all times and that I brought to individuals struggling to fit in the norm.

We are fortunate to be living at a time of great change for the LGBT community. The education system has been forced to respond to the diversity of individuals and families and I have been proud to see the positive response. My voice continues to grow and as a result have been able to develop even greater personal and professional integrity. I wish I could have found it sooner and I try not to judge myself too harshly for this. I feel blessed to be at this place and I am a stronger educator because of this process. There is no one path towards finding voice in difficult situations. Small steps do result in great gains. I would urge anyone in a similar situation to consider how to find "their voice," even in the most difficult of times. It will fill your soul.

—Barbara
Albany, New York

CONCLUSION

Gay people often know their orientation during the first 10 years of life, making them vulnerable to discrimination at a very early age. Much of civil society fails to internalize this reality. Thankfully allies exist with a greater understanding. (Gay Straight Alliance, n.d. p. 1)

The reality is that being an educator is hard work, but standing up for what is right is even harder; especially if you are an educator in a school that is resistant to change. There is the potential that you will be verbally harassed when you stand up for LGBT rights.

All who enter the school doors in the morning are entitled to a safe environment to learn, no matter their sexual orientation. It is vitally important that teachers and staff in the public school system address issues of sexual diversity with students in their class because the public school system is a microcosm of society at large, and children need to be exposed to many different lifestyles. Schools have an opportunity, and in fact, an obligation to prepare students for the outside world, where they will work with sexually diverse men and women. Students must be prepared to enter society with a more open mind, where all individuals deserve the right to be who they are, whether they are gay or straight.

As society moves forward with accepting this minority population, school districts have received support from the court systems.

"Local school districts generally have a great deal of latitude with respect to curricular content, and courts typically have rejected parental efforts to dictate or alter it" (GLSEN, 2010, p. 7). Schools, therefore, have created policies that address the need to teach controversial topics, which provides educators with the academic freedom they deserve, so they can fairly educate our youth on topics they need to know for their future.

"Leaders in all organizations, whether they know it or not, contribute for better or for worse to moral purpose in their own organizations and in society as a whole" (Fullen, 2001, p. 15). Without the assistance and support of a school leader, many teachers find it difficult to broach the topic of sexual diversity, which creates a domino effect because sexually diverse students who go unsupported have a more difficult time in school. Their peer relationships can suffer, which leads to a lack of engagement in school. Lack of engagement has negative effects on grades and the whole school experience.

Fullen cites Von Krogh and colleagues, stating, "A culture of care is vital for successful performance, which they define in five dimensions: mutual trust, active empathy, access to help, lenience in judgment, and courage" (2001, p. 82). All five dimensions are important to the issue of sexual diversity. Schools need these dimensions when considering safeguards for these students.

Action Steps

- Create a supportive learning environment in your classroom or school. This concept starts from the top down. A building without proper policies and codes of conduct are not supportive. Include all groups into the policies because they deserve an equal opportunity in your school regardless of whether school staff agrees with their lifestyle.
- Educate staff about bullying and LGBT issues. Staff may not know anyone who is gay, so they need exposure to the group so they can build awareness on how to help.
- Implement a bullying program in your school. A quality bullying program must include staff, students, administration, parents, and the community that surrounds the school. People do not buy into canned programs, but they do buy into philosophies.
- Participate in GLSEN's "No Name Calling Week" in your elementary, middle, or high school. "No Name Calling Week" is a simple idea with a powerful message. Visit www.glsen.org for more details. The website offers print copies and other resources that are age appropriate.

(Continued)

- Participate in GLSEN's Safe Space Campaign. LGBT students need to know where the supportive teachers are in the building, and this campaign offers triangles to stick on the door so students can identify those supportive teachers.
- Have teachers stand at the doorway during student transitions along with hall monitors who patrol the hallways. Bullying happens mostly in unstructured areas. Try to minimize the unstructured areas.
- Read literature that includes racial, economic, and sexual diversity in your classroom or school. Find books that have gay characters that are woven into the storyline. The less diverse your school, the more important these books are to exposing your students to the diversity of the real world.
- Hang posters and student art in the hallways that focus on diversity.
- Involve your student population in the It Gets Better Campaign. For more information, go to www.itgetsbetter.org.
- Empower students to stand up for themselves and for others, and teach students the coping skills to deal with being bullied. We need to try to do something about kids who are being bullied but we need the kids being bullied to know we care.
- Have students create Public Service Announcements to end bullying in your school.
- Allow students to include sexual orientation in their antibullying campaign.
- Do not give up on stopping bullying. The alternative to giving up is much worse.

Discussion Questions

- How can your school better address the needs of LGBT students?
- Does your school have a bullying issue?
- Why is it important to create an antibullying climate in your school? Not just for LGBT students, but an antibullying climate for all students?
- Does your school leader feel that the bullying of LGBT students is a serious issue?
    - If yes, how can you help your school leader better address the issue?
    - If no, how can you get your school leader to deal with this issue?
- If you have an antibullying program in your school, how is it being utilized?
- How can you involve all students in an antibullying campaign?
- If you have a student who is questioning their gender in school, how do you help them?

(Continued)

(Continued)

- How would your school community feel if you began an antibullying campaign that included LGBT students?
- How long do you think it takes to change the climate in a school building?
- What ideas do you have that will help change your school climate?

CHAPTER THREE

The Role of Schools

W hat is the role of the school? Why do parents send their kids to us? What do we all want our students and children to look like when they leave high school? There is a strong push to cultivate and educate the whole child. The whole child includes more than reading and math; it also includes fostering art, music, and athletics, and it should include educating students about the real world.

As educators, we know students need to be exposed to other cultures, races, and groups that they will meet as they enter college or the workforce. Lesbian, gay, bisexual, and transgender (LGBT) students and adults are one such group our students need more exposure to because they are in every community and every college across North America. "Not only is high school culture not tolerant of sexual minorities, it is complicit in tolerance, violence, and murder, and coming out may be out-right dangerous" (Savage & Harley, 2009, p. 2).

We are simply not meeting the needs of all of our students. Academically we have students leave us who struggled throughout their formal education, and they are convinced we were not there to help. Those struggling students believe we exist to help the high-achieving students succeed and feel we ignore their needs. Not only do we lose students, but we lose parents who get frustrated with us because we could not help their children, regardless of whether they took responsibility in the growth and development of their children through support at home. "Both the quality and equity of schools depend greatly on the quality of the relationships among teachers and students' and their communities" (Agirdag & Van Houtte, 2011, p. 42).

It takes the whole community to change the culture of a school. That community can be involved in stifling a school culture and making it worse, or it can be instrumental in changing the school culture for the better. A positive school culture that is not afraid to address LGBT issues can help all students feel accepted, and help our young adults grow as people and as learners. "The experiences of invisibility and isolation with which LGBTQ youngsters contend in their homes and in the community at-large extend to the school setting, as well" (Savage & Harley, 2009, p. 5).

It's not possible to address problems without being able to talk about them. To fully and effectively combat the LGBT-related harassment that persists in schools, all members of the school community must be able to discuss the topic openly, in a courteous, respectful, and professional manner, and in all possible settings. (Biegel, 2011, p. 21)

WAYS TO CHANGE THE SCHOOL CULTURE

- Begin using inclusive language such as gay, lesbian, bisexual, and transgendered. Adults often do not say the words out loud in conversation.
- Create a Principal's Advisory Council (PAC) and make creating a positive school climate your primary goal. A PAC would include a student, teacher from each subject-level, parent, and administrator. PAC should have a chair and cochair who are not administrators.
- Make school climate one of your primary goals when meeting with your PTA/PTO.

THE IMPACT SCHOOLS CAN HAVE ON LGBT STUDENTS

Schools often find themselves in the position of playing many roles in the lives of the students that walk in their doors. School staff play the role of educator, parent, and role models for our students, especially when those students lack the positive influence at home that would normally fill those roles. When it comes to LGBT students, school personnel can proactively deal with the negative realities that these students face and can have a positive impact on the LGBT community. Education and awareness help make a positive impact and will change some of these negative issues regarding this minority group of students. Creating policies, using sexually diverse literature that depicts same-sex couples in a positive way, and offering groups such as gay–straight alliances (GSA) can help foster a more positive attitude toward sexually diverse students. Unfortunately, many schools do not offer these supports, and sexually diverse students often feel very alone.

> Educators must continue to move away from seeing gay as unmentionable in school settings. Indeed the assumption that the word is not currently mentioned is a misconception. It's in fact mentioned in schools all the time, but often in a negative way. Bottom line: The simple mention of words describing LGBT people in a neutral fashion—can play a big part in countering antigay sentiment and enabling our public schools to help point the way toward a better future for everyone. (Biegel, 2011, p. 21)

The pressure schools face when including sexually diverse topics is sometimes too great for educators and administrators to take on when they have a long list of other issues to deal with, such as declining enrollment, closing of school buildings, economic hardships, common core standards, and teacher and administrator evaluation. However, the reality is that including LGBT safeguards and curriculum is not "heavy lifting" compared with the aforementioned issues. To use those issues as a reason not to confront LGBT issues is merely an excuse. The following vignette sheds some light on how uncomfortable a conversation about LGBT students can be.

Vignette

Uncomfortable Conversation

We create a niche for all students whether in the GSA, various club and extracurricular activities. Methodology in this school is to deal with acceptance and understanding for all people. Within that window are a lot of people who are traditionally marginalized. A couple of weeks ago we were meeting with parents to discuss risky business and sexual promiscuity among students. It was powerful and dynamic because it was more of a discussion than a lecture. A parent raised her hand and asked how we were addressing sexual

(Continued)

(Continued)

promiscuity amongst gay youth. I realized at the moment that we were only talking about heterosexual students. When she asked the question you could feel the discomfort in the room. It made me think about how many times we take it for granted and we have a lot of work to be done in terms of specific needs.

—DeWitt, 2010, p. 47

Without addressing the needs of LGBT students, educators are not addressing the needs of all students. Educators must include LGBT students in their conversations.

KEEPING STUDENTS SAFE

"I knew I was queer when I was a small child. My voice was gentle and sweet. I avoided sports and all roughness. I played with girls" (Rofes, 1995, p. 79). Eric Rofes's depiction of himself is one example of the plight of LGBT students in the public school system. However, in the elementary and middle school, teachers often have difficulties finding ways for students to fit in. Rofes goes on to state what can happen to these children who do not fit in with their peers.

As I got older and fully entered the society of children, I met the key enforcer of social roles among children: the bully. The bully was the boy who defined me as queer to my peers. If they had not already noticed, he pointed out my non-conformity. He was ever-present throughout my childhood, like an evil spirit entering different bodies on different occasions. (Rofes, 1995, p. 79)

Rofes's depiction of his fear of torment in school is a good example of why it is important for school personnel to step in and help safeguard this "at-risk" population. Offering safeguards helps the sexually diverse students know they are protected and tells bullies that their negative actions will not be tolerated.

People who identify themselves as gay or coming out do not have a variety of places to turn for assistance. "LGBTQ children and adolescents face a number of other risks to their physical and mental health secondary to the attitudes expressed toward their sexual orientations" (Savage & Harley, 2009, p. 6). If the right school leader is involved, it is important that schools show the same support to LGBT students that they do for any other students going through difficult times. Rofes (1995) states, "Teachers and administrators must play an active role in interrupting bullying. No longer should teachers pretend that this kind of persecution is not taking place and that boys who are named sissies are themselves at fault for their predicament" (p. 83).

TEACHER BIASES

In a small study of nine elementary school teachers in Los Angeles, Gabriel Flores investigated teacher attitudes toward gay-themed literature, focusing on the importance of incorporating a diverse curriculum in schools. He concluded the following:

> A goal of multicultural education is to accomplish the development of togetherness among people through knowledge, skills, and positive attitudes that are imperative for dealing with diversity and may foster mutual relationships and a harmonious coexistence between people of different cultures. Schools are the most effective place for educating minds toward a pluralistic society. (Flores, 2009, p. 59)

Whether we like it or not, many of our students come from homes that teach ignorance and hatred. Other households do not foster openness and acceptance, and many students come from homes where children and their parents have not been exposed to other cultures or minority groups. Some of those parents choose not to expose their children to diversity, and others live in communities that lack a great deal of diversity. School may be the only place where these students are exposed to cultures and people who are different than they are.

In order to make sure that students learn about other cultures and minorities in a correct way, administrators and teachers must make sure that they are teaching about those groups properly. One way school staff can make sure that they are teaching in a correct manner is to do research to make sure they understand the groups enough to teach others. In addition, especially where the LGBT community is concerned, staff must make sure they are teaching free of biases, which is very difficult to do. However, they need to be reflective and honest enough to admit, at least to themselves, that they have biases toward the groups they are going to teach about. It's not that having biases is acceptable, but the reality is that we all have biases about other groups. Those biases may come from a lack of exposure or overexposure to a group. When we are not always exposed to a group of people, or perhaps we are constantly confronted by a group of people, we create biases in our own minds. Besides community pressure, biases of a group are one of the biggest roadblocks to educating students about LGBT issues.

PROFESSIONAL DEVELOPMENT

How do we educate our educators on issues that LGBT students face? How do we teach them about properly addressing student issues with LGBT families? The best way to educate teachers, staff, and administrators about the issues the LGBT community face is through professional development. Professional development, when done correctly, can provide important insight for our teaching staff.

Hirsch (2007) studied the attitudes of 206 preservice teachers. She states, "respondents generally reported moderately positive attitudes toward sexual minorities" (Hirsch, 2007, p. 43). This has implications for sexually diverse students because it means many people entering the teaching profession have a positive attitude toward sexual minorities and may be more likely to have positive interactions with sexually diverse students. Hirsch (2007) also found that there was a large majority of people who hold nonhomophobic feelings and a very small percentage (15.6%) of people who do hold homophobic feelings toward sexual minorities. Although this was a small sample, the implications of it are important because it researched the attitudes of people who will be working day to day with sexual minority students, and how these people feel about students based on students' sexual orientation.

Research related to professional development training for teachers who must deal with LGBT issues is scarce, but organizations such as the Gay Lesbian Straight Education Network (GLSEN) are setting the standard for addressing these issues. GLSEN's research shows that school leaders believe there needs to be more professional development in the area of teaching educators about the needs of sexually diverse students. In its 2008 Principal Survey, 1,580 K–12 school leaders were surveyed, and GLSEN found the following:

> Professional development addressing lesbian, gay or bisexual student issues and transgender issues emerges as another unmet need among principals. Only 4% of principals reported that their school provides training for staff on LGBT issues. However, one-quarter (24%) of principals indicate that LGBT student issues are among the areas where staff need the most support or training and two in ten principals (20%) indicate that teachers need the most support and training on transgender issues. (p. 69)

In many areas around the country, there are LGBT Community Centers or nonprofits that focus on LGBT issues, which can all be used as a resource for schools when providing professional development to teachers and staff. Unfortunately, there are fewer than 100 LGBT community centers in the United States and Canada, which means that this vital resource is not always available to schools around North America. Therefore, schools need to have a resource person such as an administrator, counselor, psychologist, or teacher that can do the research for them and provide turnkey training to staff.

Vignette

The Pride Center

The Pride Center of the Capital Region is the oldest continuously operating lesbian, gay, bisexual, and transgender (LGBT) community center in the country, founded in 1970. We originated as a safe space for LGBT community members and have since expanded to provide a full range of programs and services for LGBT people of all ages in 10 counties in upstate New York. These services include a nightly drop-in center, social and support groups, low-cost counseling, senior support, and a comprehensive youth program. Over 26 years ago, the Pride Center began the Center Youth program for LGBT youth ages 13 to 18. This program now works with more than 600 young people each year, and more than 200 school districts to ensure safe learning environments. The youth of our community are the most vulnerable, so specific attention is
(Continued)

(Continued)

directed at ensuring a supportive environment for LGBT youth to be supported to foster resilience, leadership and pride.

In addition to working directly with LGBT youth, the Pride Center is the coordinator of the Capital Region Safe Schools Coalition. This coalition is a consortium of schools throughout the Capital Region committed to creating safe and welcoming environments for all students to learn. To expand upon the coalition's work, the Pride Center has created the Center Youth Action Team, an exceptional group of young people who have committed their time and energy to conduct speaking engagements in schools to create more welcoming learning environments in the Capital Region. These students are catalysts for change for other youth to create more compassionate and respectful school climates for themselves and their peers.

The Center Youth Action Team uses a peer-based model that has proven effective for meaningful interventions with youth. There are many benefits to this project as it conducts free trainings on a range of LGBT and general youth issues for schools and community groups throughout the year. It supports schools in creating welcoming learning environments for all of their students by training teachers, students, and administrators on the unique issues facing LGBT youth. In addition to the benefit to the larger community, the program provides Team member youth with training and speaking opportunities to help develop a sense of confidence and pride in their identities. The Center Youth Action Team is designed to encourage youth leadership, contradict myths and stereotypes of the LGBT community, and provide positive representations of the LGBT community.

Intervention in incidents of bullying by supportive educators can significantly improve the educational outcomes for LGBT students and reduce the incidence of anti-LGBT bullying, harassment, and name-calling. Not only is effective intervention related to decreased levels of in-school victimization, but research demonstrates that LGBT students who can identify supportive school staff report a greater sense of safety at school, skip school less often, perform better academically, and have a stronger commitment to continuing their education through high school and beyond.

The Capital Region Safe Schools Project, a multilevel initiative, currently works with school personnel and student groups in more than 30 schools to make local schools safe for all youth. Key components of the Capital Region Safe Schools Project include "Best Practices" policy development assistance for administrators, and a comprehensive toolkit of available trainings and seminars on a range of issues related to LGBT youth, including LGBT 101, Trans 101, LGBT Youth Ally Building, and Supporting LGBT Families. We provide more than 60 free trainings each year to schools in order to equip teacher and administrators with the skills they need to become advocates for their LGBT students. In addition to teacher training, a vital part of the Safe Schools Project is the Center Youth Action Team, a diverse speaker's bureau of exceptional group of young people who have committed their time and energy who travel to local schools telling their stories and facilitating dialogue on how to make schools more welcoming in the Capital Region. They are catalysts *for other youth to create more compassionate and respectful school environments for their peers.*

The program theory of the Safe Schools Project is designed to be a multilevel intervention to improve the social, emotional, and academic outcomes for LGBT youth in schools. The goal is to influence educator awareness and knowledge of issues that LGBT youth face to result in increased and strengthened intervention when LGBT youth are targeted in schools for real or perceived LGBT identity. The improved school personnel behaviors will be supported by inclusive policies from administration that reinforce the behaviors on a daily basis.

The youth participating in the Center Youth Action Team develop their skills in public speaking, group facilitation and presentation giving. Those who receive the Center Youth Action Team's presentations, such as local school classrooms, teachers, youth serving agency staff, and students, will have an increased understanding of the issues that LGBT youth face and gain the tools needed to create more welcoming environments for LGBT youth in the future.

—Nora Yates, Executive Director

Vignette

Rainbow Resource Centre

The Rainbow Resource Centre (RRC) has existed in Winnipeg, MB, Canada, since 1973. Currently, we provide various services and supports to the LGBTQ community in Winnipeg, throughout Manitoba, and to Northwestern Ontario. Services include counseling services—drop-in counseling; individual counseling; couples counseling; family counseling; and various closed counseling groups offered throughout the year; youth programming twice a week as well as a drop-in day on the weekends; volunteer opportunities with the Centre and at community events; a lending library specifically focused on queer/LGBTQ materials; community computer with Internet access; in-house programming and events for community members; and an education program. All services offered at the Centre are free for community members, their families, and for community allies.

The RRC sees education as one of the primary routes to create change in society. By providing accurate information, challenging stereotypes, and providing resources, we are able to equip workshop participants with knowledge, skills, and abilities. While not all workshop participants are open or ready to change, the great majority (90% +) provide outstanding feedback on the knowledge they've gained and on the process and participation they experience within workshops. Our education program typically delivers between 100 to 130 anti-homophobia education workshops a year. Primary areas of delivery are within the public school system [K–12]; social service agencies; health care workers; private businesses and workplaces; and students in postsecondary education. Workshops are developed to meet the specific needs of target audiences/ages.

(Continued)

(Continued)

Using current research and evidence-based practices, workshops provide relevant training and information by matching content to the audience (i.e., best health care practices for health care professionals; combating bullying/homophobia in school settings for teachers and education students; creating alliances in therapeutic relationships for counselors/social workers and school psychologists). One of our recent developments in our education program is the use of peer education to create change in schools and classroom cultures.

The YEAH program (Youth Education Against Homophobia) utilizes trained volunteer facilitators between the ages of 17 to 25 to deliver peer education. Workshops are structured from an hour to 90 minutes in length and utilize an anti-oppressive education approach to engage participants in activities, discussions, and awareness-raising regarding the impacts of homophobia and the connections of different oppressions, such as racism, sexism, ableism, etc. All YEAH facilitators are provided with an honorarium for their time in training sessions (16 hours of training) and for workshops they facilitate.

Compensation for their time is important, as YEAH workshops ask peers to step up and share their own experiences and stories; our intent is never to exploit youth facilitators, but to empower them in the change process within school cultures. All YEAH facilitators are accompanied by an RRC staff person who is there to support them in their workshop delivery and assist if workshop participants are disengaged, hostile, or difficult. Our belief is that the peer-to-peer education model is extremely effective but can come with many challenges in having peers deliver training to their peers. Launched in the spring of 2011, the YEAH education model has been extremely effective and in high demand, with teachers also recognizing the impact of peer-led education.

—*Chad Smith, MSW*
Executive Director, Rainbow Resource Centre

PARENT OUTREACH

No one is more important to a child than his or her parents. Having open and accepting parents can set LGBT children on a positive course through life. Unfortunately, not all parents accept their children when they come out. This rejection can have negative effects on an LGBT child's future.

Gay and transgender teens who were highly rejected by their parents and caregivers are at very high risk for health and mental health problems when they become young adults (ages 21–25). Highly rejected young people are:

- More than 8 times as likely to have attempted suicide,
- Nearly 6 times as likely to report high levels of depression,
- More than 3 times as likely to use illegal drugs, and
- More than 3 times as likely to be at high risk for HIV and sexually transmitted diseases (Ryan, 2009, p. 5).

Schools can play a vital role in the road to acceptance between parents and their LGBT child. This is, of course, a very sensitive subject among schools and parents. "Obviously, educators need to exercise care when discussing LGBT students—some may not be 'out' to family members, or some parents and caregivers may not be supportive of their children's LGBT identities" (Sadowski, 2010, p. 12). How do we, as educators, know when we are over-stepping our boundaries with parents? When does the school go too far in its advocacy for an LGBT student? Typically, when a student who is questioning whether he or she is gay or straight seeks the help of an adult, a school counselor should step in as a reference for the teacher in order to best help the student. Many LGBT students feel more comfortable telling a teacher if they do not have a supportive home life. This teacher needs to bridge the gap between the parent and the child. However, some parents still may not feel comfortable with their child coming out, and school staff members can choose to find resources for the child in case that happens. As educators, we try to be there for our students, and there are times that the best thing we can do is give them the resources they need so they can learn how to best deal with their feelings and advocate for themselves.

Parents of LGBT children go through a variety of stages when their children come out to them. Just like stages of grief that people go through when a loved one dies, parents go through stages where they are shocked, angry, saddened, and finally learn to accept their LGBT children. However, the Family Acceptance Program (FAP) at San Francisco State University has found in a study (2009) that 42% of LGBT students have families that reject them. Rejection can take place for a number of reasons, but one of the biggest factors is a lack of understanding of what being gay really means.

Groups such as FAP offer services to families to increase the level of understanding and therefore the level of acceptance. Unfortunately, there are few organizations like FAP around North America. Schools could help fill the void by offering information to the parents of LGBT students.

CONCLUSION

Schools need to find a balance when educating students. They need to take on the role of exposing students to a diverse world, provoking thought, and educating them about the world around them. Many students only experience the world through the Internet and do not always have the opportunity to see life for the place that it is until they leave their home and go off to college or the workforce.

As much as the Internet offers students a window into the world around them, it does not always educate them in a proper way. The Internet offers possibilities, but it is not always safe, and students need the support of adults to guide them through the usual storm and stress of young adulthood. Parents are the adults who offer the largest impact on children, but sometimes kids do not feel as though they can confide in their parents because they feel they may be rejected. Being rejected is hard enough, but being rejected by one's own parents can have devastating results.

Teachers and administrators offer students hope, and that is especially true for LGBT students. In a world that can seem very lonely, hearing the word gay or being introduced to characters and literature that have a gay character or theme can be a step toward acceptance. Teachers need to expose students to diversity without the biases they may have hidden inside. Administrators need to make those teachers who are brave enough to broach the subject of LGBT issues feel safe so they can best reach those LGBT students.

Parents have choices. They can choose to ignore the fact that their child is gay. They can choose to have their child pulled from a class that includes LGBT topics. They can even choose to keep their children home on days when schools participate in the Day of Silence or other events that focus on LGBT issues.

Good schools provoke though even in times when they may receive criticism. Those schools that stand up for LGBT students are putting themselves at risk, but our best social justice leaders always put themselves at risk because they know what they are doing is right, no matter the consequences. Our job as educators is to educate those who walk in our doors and, sometimes, that includes parents as well.

Action Steps

- Encourage your superintendent to include the same inclusive language in school board policies. School board policies give building principals the leverage they need when disciplining students.
- Have conversations with parents at PTA meetings about fostering a more positive school climate.
- Offer resources on your school website that will provide tips to parents about how to spot bullying.
- Offer professional development to teachers, such as a guest speaker from a local gay and lesbian community center.
- Do not be afraid to say the word "gay" out loud. Often adults whisper the word as if something were wrong with it.
- An inclusive school that promotes a safe climate is not catering to LGBT students. It is actually allowing all students to feel welcome.

Discussion Questions

- What do you believe is the role the school system should play in the lives of LGBT students?
- Do you feel schools overstep their boundaries when they expose students to LGBT curriculum?
- Who should make curricular decisions for schools?
- How would parents feel about having a gay and lesbian community center working with your school?
- What are your biases about LGBT students or the LGBT community?
- What types of professional development do you believe staff need in the area of LGBT issues?

CHAPTER FOUR

Curriculum Matters

When we open a good book and read about a character that we identify with, it's like the weight of the world goes away and everything around us is going to be all right. Everyone needs an escape from their daily lives. Turning on the television, reading books, or seeing billboards as we drive to work or school exposes us to a variety of images that are predominately heterosexual. Where are the homosexual images that can help lesbian, gay, bisexual, and transgender (LGBT) kids and adults feel normal? The hidden curriculum is that being heterosexual is normal and being gay should be hidden. The reality is that there are many people who feel that way, including politicians who use it as a platform to run on for office. "Promoting awareness would curb antigay stereotypes and thereby reduce bullying of and violence against lesbian, gay, bisexual, and transgendered students (Robelen, 2011, p. 10).

In 2010, the In Our Own Voices organization began a campaign titled "I Am Gay," and there were several billboards promoting the campaign around the Albany, New York, area. The billboards had several African-American men and women on them. The idea of the billboard was to bring awareness to the AIDS epidemic, which plagues the African-American community. By having the billboards, In Our Own Voices wanted to take the stigma away from being gay in the African-American community, and therefore perhaps more men and women would stop engaging in risky behavior that they have to hide. The ultimate goal for this campaign would be to raise self-esteem in the community so LGBT men and women would be out, open, and safe, which would bring down the inordinate number of people with HIV in the African-American LGBT community.

Some local politicians and community members were infuriated with the campaign and stated that In Our Voices was a gay movement that was putting the gay lifestyle "in the faces" of residents. A politician appeared on the news and said that the campaign made it sound as though being gay was all right, and that In Our Own Voices was promoting that message to the community. The organization was interviewed after the politician's remarks and said he was correct. The message they wanted the community to get from the campaign was indeed that being gay was all right and should not be hidden.

Living in the Albany area, I commute every day to work and began taking a more focused look at the billboards that run next to 787 and I90, which are both major highways in the Capital District area. It was interesting that no one spoke up about the billboards that promote participating in the lottery (gambling), the numerous drinking billboards that contribute to alcoholism, or the billboards that promoted the local strip clubs. These images are so accepted in our society that we are desensitized to them. However, two billboards promoting the acceptance of gays and lesbians are appalling to some people.

We as educators can find ways to introduce LGBT related topics in school. One of the easiest and most unobtrusive ways to introduce LGBT topics in the classroom is through the use of literature. Literature can expose students to the topic in a thought-provoking way.

DIVERSE LITERATURE AT AN AGE-APPROPRIATE LEVEL

From kindergarten through high school, there are many books that show characters that are either gay or live in a home with gay parents. These are important characters and families for children and teenagers to see for a variety of reasons. If a student is gay or living in a family with gay parents, these books provide a familiar setting. If the students listening to the story are neither gay nor are they growing up in a family with gay parents, the books provide important exposure to diverse families.

Books that appropriately expose children to sexually diverse families have been a controversial topic because conservatives and religious groups believe that books that have a theme of introducing sexually diverse families or characters are pushing the gay agenda. Whether these groups agree or not, there are a percentage of students who do not identify with the nuclear family and deserve to read about families such as their own. School is the important venue for this because these LGBT families are involved in the school system.

> The American Library Association's (ALA) Office for Intellectual Freedom only documents written challenges to library books and materials (there were 420 cases in 2007), and even then, it estimates that only one out of five cases are reported. But when it comes to self-censorship, it's almost impossible to quantify because no one is monitoring it or collecting stats, and there's no open discussion on the subject. (Whelan, 2009, p. 1)

Vignette

Book Banning

I suspected that there would be some concern about the gay character named Pan in my book, Magic and Misery. *And I knew it was something of a risk for the main character, TJ, to have her first sexual experience with a boy, especially without its resulting in her pregnancy or HIV contraction, or in a bout of hysterical crying. Perhaps the candor between TJ and her gay best friend would ruffle some feathers. Even before the book was sold, my agent warned me that certain publishers would not take kindly to its sexual forthrightness.*

But there are tons of books for teenagers with far more explicit sexual situations, and there are hundreds of LGBT-themed young adult novels. Magic and Misery *received all kinds of good press, a starred review in* Booklist, *being named to that publication's Top Ten Books for Young Adults, and the ALA Round Table, which selected it for its 2010 bibliography. A raft of online bloggers' reviews ranged from positive to raves. But a writer only pays attention to the bad reviews. We survive them, even when that doesn't at first seem like an option. I knew the usual demographic wouldn't like the book, no accolades from* Christianity Today, *for example. But I was not prepared for the latent homophobia in some of the responses. One reviewer for an influential publication commented on the "cringe worthy homophobia" that the gay teen experienced, the insinuation being that what he experienced was over-the-top, manufactured. Another reviewer actually blamed the boy for bringing on the torment he was subjected to. And one critic posited that the gay character was so enamored of his straight girl best friend that parents should be concerned about the positive portrayal of a potential stalker. Oy.*

(Continued)

(Continued)

Truthfully, lots of school librarians bought the book and championed it in their institutions and online. Before the book's release I had joked that I wanted someone to challenge my novel so it would sell more copies, maybe get a few minutes on Oprah. But in order to be challenged, a book has to get into public places, and this was my introduction to the concept of soft censoring. Soft censoring is where librarians and teachers avoid what they predict to be inevitable conflicts by simply not buying a book in the first place. For the first time I truly understood how school librarians and language arts teachers are on the front lines of the censorship battle, how part of their job description is defending and fighting to keep relevant books in their libraries. Several librarian friends and acquaintances of mine told me they would not buy Magic and Misery *because they could already see the fight they would be embroiled in: a book with an unapologetic gay male teenager who jokes about sex, and a girl who has her first sexual experience and speaks candidly with her gay best friend about it. I finally saw the reality of their daily working lives: dealing with nervous administrators, volleying with aggressive parents who would accuse them of trying to turn their children into sluts and homosexuals. And then it came back to me: When I taught secondary English in the 1980s, I did soft-censoring all the time, even avoided authors—when I had a grant to bring them into the school—who would elicit controversy. Even as a college professor I have treaded lightly with material with gay themes, often announcing verbally and in my syllabus a disclaimer that includes an opt-out option (though the option is dropping the course).*

And any author gets the poison-penned emails. One admirer wanted to know why there were such books for teens "with rotten morals." Another wrote, "Don't you people write about anything else? You're obsessed with this gay stuff." These were to be expected. But the other issues took me by surprise. I learned a hard and important lesson—about the resilience of the old fears, prejudices, and assumptions, no matter how often they are beaten back.

—Peter Marino, Author

Although it seems surprising that books are still being banned, whether publicly or silently through the use of self-censorship, this widely accepted practice happens on a daily basis, and gay-themed books are often the genre that is at the heart of self-censorship. There are numerous reasons why this genre is often banned. "In the first survey of its kind, *School Library Journal* (*SLJ*) recently asked 655 media specialists about their collections and found that 70 percent of librarians say they won't buy certain controversial titles simply because they're terrified of how parents will respond" (Whelan, 2009, p. 2).

The following vignette offers one of the many reasons why librarians and teachers will not read LGBT-related books in the classroom.

Banning Families

All first-grade teachers in the ACS school district read the book titled Families *by Meredith Tax because it is a book on their curriculum list. The book, which was published in the early 1980s, is a picture book where the setting of the story takes place on an elementary school playground. Children out at recess begin talking about who they live with at home. Some of the children live with both parents, some live in two homes because their parents are divorced, a few live with grandparents, and one child lives with her mother and godmother.*

After Mrs. Choukeir, a teacher in the Naylor School, read Families, *a parent complained that the school was pushing homosexuality. The parents argued that the book focused on a little girl living with her gay parents. Mrs. Choukeir tried several times to explain to the parents complaining that the little girl lived with her mother and godmother and it does not specifically state that the child lives with gay parents. After numerous e-mails back and forth the principal, Dr. O'Brien, stepped in and asked to meet with the parents. The parents met with Dr. O'Brien and he explained that the book did not push homosexuality, but the parents wanted it banned from first grade. Dr. O'Brien went on to explain that even if the book did include a lesbian family, he would allow the book to be used anyway because there were several gay parents in the school. This fact seemed to surprise the parents looking to ban the book. The parents spent 30 minutes trying to get Dr. O'Brien to understand why the book needed to be banned. He ended the meeting by stating that the parents had very conservative private school views and that would end up being a problem in the school because it is a public school and they teach about awareness and do not want any group to feel unaccepted in their school.*

After meeting with Dr. O'Brien, they went to the Assistant Superintendent of Curriculum and Instruction to ask her to form a committee to look at the relevancy of the book and possibly ban it. The ACS school district had a board policy that stated that parents could ask for such a committee to protect children from controversial curriculum. None of the teachers from the Naylor School using the book would be allowed to join the committee because there was a fear that Dr. O'Brien may force them to side with his opinion. After much deliberation the committee supported Dr. O'Brien's decision and the book continued to be used in all of the elementary schools.

The parents, per board policy, were allowed to bring it to the "next level," which meant that they could bring it directly to the board. The board agenda went out a few days before the meeting and one of the items on the agenda was the decision to ban the book or keep it used in the classrooms. Numerous community members attended the meeting, most of them showed up to make sure their school district would not ban the book.

(Continued)

(Continued)

The board began to discuss Families *and made the decision to support Dr. O'Brien and allow the book to be used in first grade. The parents left the board meeting stating that they felt that the school district went far beyond its boundaries with families and curriculum. However, they did not take their child out of the Naylor School.*

The previous vignette is a true story but the names have been changed to protect the real participants in the story. Book banning, although many would feel is a thing of the past, is still happening around North America. Hopefully more courageous educators will stand up and go against the grain. See the box on this page for a list of some books that have an LGBT theme.

LGBT-THEMED BOOKS

- *Christian, the Hugging Lion* by Justin Richardson and Peter Parnell, illustrated by Amy June Bates (Simon & Schuster)
- *God Loves Hair* by Vivek Shraya, illustrated by Juliana Neufeld
- *Jumpstart the World* by Catherine Ryan Hyde (Random House Books for Children)
- *Wildthorn* by Jane Eagland (Houghton Mifflin Harcourt)
- *Will Grayson, Will Grayson* by John Green and David Levithan (Penguin)
- *Freaks and Revelations* by Davida Wills Hurwin (Little, Brown & Co.)
- *Love Drugged* by James Klise (Flux)
- *The Boy in the Dress* by David Walliams, illustrated by Quentin Blake (Razorbill)
- *Momma, Mommy and Me* by Lesléa Newman and illustrated by Carol Thompson (Tricycle Press)
- *Daddy, Papa and Me* by Lesléa Newman and illustrated by Carol Thompson (Tricycle Press)
- *My Princess Boy* by Cheryl Kilodavis, illustrated by Suzanne DeSimone (Aladdin)
- *Magic and Misery* by Peter Marino (Holiday House)
- *And Tango Makes Three* by Justin Richardson, illustrated by Peter Parnell (Simon & Schuster Children's Publishing)

These are only a few of the titles available. Please see your local independent book seller, book chain, or Internet-based book company for more examples.

Supportive Learning Environments for LGBT Students

Teaching children to be critical of oppression is teaching true morality, and teachers have the right, indeed the obligation, to alert their students to all forms of oppression. Educating children not to be homophobic is one way to show the difference between oppressive and non-oppressive behavior. (Gordon, 1995, p. 40)

Szalacha states, "A key factor in studies of school climate has been optimal school size: one that is best at attaining a climate that enables all members of the school community to teach and learn at optimal levels" (2001, p. 12). Edwards says, "Whether we realize it or not, we as educators are dealing with a hidden minority of gay and lesbian students, as well as gay and lesbian parents" (1997, p. 68). This "hidden minority" that Edwards refers to are looking for supportive learning environments. The nuclear family has increasingly changed over the past 20 years, and schools are inhabited by sexually diverse students as well as parents who were once married trying to identify as heterosexual.

One of the issues that come with the increasing number of LGBT students and parents entering the school system is how educators can address homosexuality. It is critical that these LGBT students and parents are educated in an environment that supports them, but often schools do not know how to address the issue because of a lack of professional development and literature on the topic of sexually diverse students. Sears states, "Too many educators are partners in the conspiracy of silence in which sexual knowledge is what is salvaged after the scissors-and-paste philosophy of religious zealots or anti-homosexual activists apply" (1991, p. 55). O'Conor states, "Discussions of heterosexism, homophobia, and the lives of lesbian, gay, and bisexual youth have been noticeably absent in the educational literature" (1995, p. 95). It is an uncomfortable subject that too many educators are scared to cover. The following vignette offers an easy way to include LGBT literature in your school.

A New Chapter for All Students

Everyone is a reader. Even the ones who claim to have not read a book throughout their high school career. When they finally HAVE to read a book and they come dragging into the library, I want to be able to provide them with a book that will "hook" them. It may be only the minimum requirement of 100 pages, but if just the right book falls into their hands, perhaps a life-long reader has been created. They may not admit it, but perhaps they've met characters who speak to them, characters they can live vicariously through, characters they can witness making teenager mistakes, characters they can cheer for.

We all want to read about people like ourselves. In the high school library, we have the books about the bad boys, the sluts, the misfits, the mean girls, the smart kids who think they're dumb, sick people, abused people, superheroes, kids who are invisible or feel that way, people who populated history, vampires and witches, kids in jail, even dead people. Up until just a few years ago, there were very few books written with gay and questioning teen characters. Our school is lucky. Our library shelves are now populated by LGBT teens as well. We have an administration and board of education that created and continue to support a library book selection policy.

Our district selection policy allows me to purchase books that "place principle above personal opinion and reason above prejudice in the selection of materials of the highest quality in order to assure a comprehensive collection appropriate for the users of the library." It's not just another dusty policy for the binder. It is supported by our principal when parents challenge book content. It is supported by the librarians in the district as they choose relevant reading material for the next generation.

When the first "gay fiction" books starting hitting our shelves, they flew out of the library. The students knew the titles, read them, and passed them along to friends. Many students who were not gay or questioning read them as well. They now had the opportunity to live vicariously through yet another kind of teenager. They learned about the pain of parental rejection and peer torment that many gay and questioning teens live with every day.

In a study done by School Library Journal *(SLJ), it was found that parents and administrators are not the only ones who censor. Librarians censor as well. When librarians know that some kinds of literature will not be supported by the adult community, they tend to censor themselves. "They tend to be skittish about book purchases for obvious reasons. Sexual content ranks number one, with 87 percent of those surveyed saying it's the main reason they shy away from buying a book. Objectionable language (61 percent) comes in second followed by violence (51 percent), homosexual themes (47 percent), racism (34 percent), and religion (16 percent)." SLJ goes on to report, "Not surprisingly, titles with gay themes get their very own category when it comes to book banning, whether self-imposed or not, because people have a very rigid, narrow view of what kinds of sexuality are allowed to exist. And oftentimes, librarians lump gay characters into the mix with sex'"* (Whelan, 2009, p. 28).

In line with the school's selection policy, I purchase books that are relevant to our student population and that are aligned with the curriculum. Often we get recommendations from students and teachers, but the vast majority of the fiction I purchase, including the "gay themed" subgenre, is through reviews. I use professional journals as well as finding new and upcoming titles initially through local bookstores, fliers, and, of course, the Internet. When someone recommends or requests a book for the library to purchase, I am duty bound by our selection policy to find and read at least one professional review before purchasing the book.

We organize our fiction in a bookstore style. We found that students came in asking "Where are the mysteries?" or "Where are the fantasy books?" and we gave them what they wanted—a library organized by genres such as Chick Fiction, Mystery, Historical Fiction, and Romance. After the change in organization, our circulation statistics skyrocketed to almost double in less than a year! Suddenly, instead of wandering aimlessly looking for the right book, kids liking the same books were standing next to each other in the "Problems" or "Mystery" section recommending books to one another and getting to know each other.

When it came to organizing our "gay fiction," we decided to incorporate them with the other genres; after all, some gay-themed books are "Romance," some are "Chick" books, and some are "Problem" books. We did not want to separate them into their own genre, just as we wouldn't want to separate our gay students from the rest of the kids. Students looking for specifically gay-themed books can look them up by title, subject, or author on the catalog, or refer to our bookmarks. We have several subgenres made into lists (war stories, gay fiction, funny books) on bookmarks displayed throughout the library. We also make up a cart of gay-themed books and bring them to the gay–straight alliance meeting for browsing.

This year, a small group of students made a great display of the gay-themed fiction books and put it by the front door of the library. It displayed books with a sign that read: "Warning: these books are gay". It was very well received. One of the philosophy classes even came down as a group to discuss it!

High school students are at an exciting, infuriating, scary time of their lives. They need relevant characters in books to experience life through—characters who can show them places they've never seen and parts of them-selves yet undiscovered.

—Patricia, School Library Media Specialist
Albany, New York

Reference

Whelan, D. A. (2009). A dirty little secret: Self-censorship is rampant and lethal. *School Library Journal, 55*(2), 27–30.

CURRICULUM

LGBT topics can be addressed in many areas in addition to literature. From political debates to historical views to discussions about famous artists and musicians, discussing LGBT topics can easily be embedded into the curriculum. Those discussions can be formal or informal, which can both be helpful. Informally adding LGBT topics that come up in discussions, such as when people use the phrase "that's so gay," can bring a sense of awareness and comfort to those involved in the conversation.

Unfortunately, sometimes formal LGBT discussions can be included in curriculum but have negative connotations. For example, many times the formal curriculum that is taught in health class focuses on the teaching of the AIDS epidemic when it comes to LGBT issues, which, stated before, is a negative stereotype of the LGBT community. However, members of the LGBT community and their allies would like to see a formal curriculum that focuses on diversity, which includes LGBT issues, because it gives them the opportunity to expose students to a diverse world.

> If schools are going to have an impact on the attitudes and behaviors of their sexually concerned and often active students, they must acknowledge in their curricula the importance of sexuality in our lives and in the lives of those who have gone before us. (Lipkin, 1995, p. 32)

The mere positive conversation about an LGBT issue can be highly important to LGBT students involved and to their heterosexual peers. If you walk around a high school setting, these conversations happen all the time with teenagers. Taking these "teachable moments" to further someone's understanding of the subject is invaluable to those who partake in the conversation. Teachers have a great deal of power with their students, whether the students tell them or not, and providing LGBT issues a place at the table can send many powerful messages. In addition, formal curriculum could have a positive impact that could last for years after the discussion.

ELEMENTARY SCHOOL GENDER DIFFERENCES AND CHARACTER EDUCATION

Boys are taught that they should play with trucks, wear blue, and steer away from dolls. G.I. Joe is not a doll; it's an army action figure, which boys are encouraged to play with because it's manly. Girls are called "tomboys" when they play sports and hang out with all boys. We grow up learning clearly defined gender roles. If a boy helps his mother in the kitchen, his friends may call him a girl when adults are not around. Children learn quickly what they can and cannot play with because they do not want to be made fun of by their peers, or worse, their siblings. In some families, parents do not want their children to be defined by gender roles, but in most families they do. It starts at infancy when little baby boys are given blue blankets and clothing and little baby girls are given pink blankets and clothing.

Bringing up these topics in an elementary school classroom is a great way to explore gender differences and create thoughtful and accepting students at a young age. Gender differences is not a gay issue, but it is a way to create a safe and nurturing atmosphere in the classroom and hopefully teach children valuable lessons that they can take as they move from grade to grade, all of which will have a large impact on bullying. I wrote the following vignette about my experience with gender roles in the classroom. It all started by mistake but it became a yearly "teachable" moment.

Vignette

Using Children's Books to Teach About Gender Differences

When I taught first grade at Arlington Elementary School in Poughkeepsie, New York, my favorite thing to do with my students was to read picture books to them at our morning calendar time. Children's picture books have the most amazing illustrations. I spent hours in our school library, with the librarian Pauline Herr. Sitting on the floor, I would ask her what books she suggested that I read to my students. We did not have the luxury of the Internet and had to use the dreaded card catalog that sat in the corner. The long brown drawers were very intimidating because they held thousands of cards in alphabetical order by category, which for the life of me I still cannot remember. Pauline would stop what she was doing and help me pull books from the shelves. I would check out about 10 books at a time and promise to hand them back in right after I used them so other teachers could take them out. She stamped my name on the card in the back of the book so she remembered that I was the one who confiscated so many at one time.

One day I took out a wordless children's picture book titled First Snow *by Emily Arnold McCully, which was written in 1988. It's a good literacy practice*

(Continued)

(Continued)

to do a "picture walk" with students before you actually read the book out loud to them. A "picture walk," although I'm sure it's called something different now, was a way to get students engaged in the book. It was considered an active reading tool as opposed to a passive reading experience, where they sat and listened but did not engage.

I remember opening First Snow *for the first time with the kids sitting on the carpet anxiously anticipating what would happen next. However, something happened that none of us expected. I opened a page to mice wearing various colored scarves. One particular mouse was wearing a pink scarf and a male student pointed to the picture and said it was a girl. When I asked him how he knew it was a girl, he said, "Because she's wearing a pink scarf," so matter-of-factly like there was something wrong with me that I could tell it was a girl. For the next 20 minutes I watched my first-grade students debate whether a boy could wear pink and whether the mouse in the story was, in fact, a girl. The boy who started the initial conversation began to cry because he was adamant that the mouse with the pink scarf was a girl.*

After many conversations and the fact that I wore a pink shirt the next day, we all agreed that girls and boys could both wear pink. Many of my parents who taught at Vassar College across the road were quite happy that I taught the lesson because they were all socially active and believed that boys and girls should not be confined to gender differences. That's the amazing thing about "teachable moments" because they come up when you do not expect them. I used the book First Snow *by Emily Arnold McCully every year so I could have the same discussion. And every day after that discussion I wore a pink shirt.*

- *In elementary school, you can have discussions with children about gender differences without ever bringing up the topic of being gay.*
- *Find books without words and do a picture walk with students, and ask thought-provoking questions where boys and girls can learn about gender differences.*
- *Books like* Free to Be You and Me *by Marlo Thomas and Christopher Cerf are perfect examples of books that teach about gender differences to children.*
- *Find examples of books where girls are doing things that are typically done by boys and vice versa.*
- *Teaching about gender differences with children does not mean you are teaching about homosexuality. It is actually a way to teach children about acceptance.*

Emily Arnold McCully, a Caldecott Medal Winner, was kind enough to provide the following vignette to explain why she believes wordless books can be so powerful for curriculum conversations.

Wordless Picture Books and Gender Expression

Picnic *is the first in a series of wordless books that actually began with words. An astute editor looked* Picnic *over and pronounced the text unnecessary. I worried, briefly, that parents might feel shortchanged. Wordless books were still rarities. But soon, I was privileged to watch a young woman tell the story in Chinese and then heard a few American youngsters working out their own versions, and it was clear that the reader can bring much more than is usual to these tales. It takes imaginative parent to make wordless books succeed. The children are already imaginative.*

As the years went by, I learned that schools in districts with many immigrants, speaking many languages, used the mouse series to teach reading. A school catering to youths who had run afoul of the law used Picnic *in junior high. The students, far from feeling condescended to, enjoyed making the narrative their own, reflecting experiences I might not have dreamed of, but that fit into the universal model that* Picnic *represents.*

Wordless books are very freeing. I wanted the gender of the little lost mouse to be the reader's choice, too. It's important to be able to identify with the protagonist as well as with the rest of the family. It confuses some, therefore, that the mouse wears a pink scarf. It must mean the character is female. The color was an impulsive choice on my part—it had to stand out in a natural setting filled with greens, blues, browns, and so on. I might have made it bright red, but that screamed Christmas. So pink it is—and pink is fine for a boy to wear. In fact, it is likely that boy readers identify with the lost mouse anyway, and so pink will open their minds to the idea that it need not be something worn only by girls.

I chose to make it an animal story to free myself as well. Humor and danger are both more easily addressed with animals. I can't imagine a publisher accepting a book that begins with a small child being pitched out of the back of a truck. To danger and humor, add gender. Much better to let animals stand for our ideas of male and female and play with them or suggest androgyny. A discussion would begin, I think, with telling the story from various points of view, comparing the experiences of all the characters.

Imagination is the root of empathy, of course. If we can put ourselves in another's shoes, that person matters. If we can do it with everyone, everyone matters. If everyone matters, there is the possibility of equality. Stories can actually produce that!

—Emily Arnold McCully, Children's Author
Caldecott Medal Winner

One other area where safeguarding LGBT students can be included is through the use of character education. Character education can help create a safe and nurturing atmosphere. Teaching words such as acceptance, caring, kindness, and respect and giving good examples of what each of those words means is a highly effective way for students to build a level of understanding for one another. Teachers can find a multitude of ways to include teachable moments in conversations about character education words so that all students can feel accepted and appreciated. A strong character education program is a vital element of all elementary schools.

ENGLISH LANGUAGE ARTS

Just like the great children's books that are used to subtly explore gender issues, middle school and high school teachers can explore LGBT topics through the use of literature. Whether it's a gay author or a book that involves a gay character, books can be an effective way to explore a multitude of topics. Teachers explore the lives of heterosexual authors all the time, so exploring the lives of homosexual authors should be done in very much the same way.

The following vignette is an example of using poetry to discuss LGBT topics in a very natural way in the classroom.

Using Poems to Provoke Thought

Because I Liked You Better
A. E. Housman

Because I liked you better
Than suits a man to say,
It irked you, and I promised
To throw the thought away.

To put the world between us
We parted, stiff and dry;
'Good-Bye', said you, 'forget me.'
'I will, no fear', said I.

If here, where the clover whitens
The dead man's knoll, you pass,

And no tall flower to meet you
Starts in the trefoiled grass,

Halt by the headstone naming
The heart no longer stirred,
And say the lad that loved you
Was one that kept his word.

From Housman, A. E., 1936.

Using poems like the one above by A. E. Housman (1936), teachers can create debate and discussion in their classroom. That particular poem was written for his college roommate Moses Jackson who was a heterosexual male, so the feelings were never reciprocated. The following are potential questions to use after reading the poem.

- Who was A. E. Housman referring to in his poem?
- Why do you think they could not take the relationship further?
- When was the poem written?
- What were times like back then for gays and lesbians?

SOCIAL STUDIES

Social studies curriculum is another area where LGBT issues can be addressed. Biegel states that "age appropriate, LGBT related material in the K–12 curriculum can range from lessons linked specifically to antibullying initiatives to social studies units on civil rights movements and legal studies units focusing on First Amendment topics" (2011, p. 21). Students can debate "don't ask, don't tell," gay marriage, and Supreme Court Decisions that affect the LGBT community. These issues often spark great debates among students, which will help lead to a better understanding of society.

See the box on page 58 for a few ways to include LGBT discussions in a social studies class. The ideas are meant to spark further ideas for teachers and administrators.

EMBEDDING LGBT ISSUES INTO SOCIAL STUDIES CURRICULUM

- In 1966, the first gay community center opened in San Francisco. What implications did that have for the country? What do you think the public perception was of the LGBT community at that time?
- In 1965, homosexuals picketed the White House. Why do you think that the LGBT community would need to picket the White House?
- In 1967, there was a CBS special titled "The Homosexual." Watch the documentary with the class and take notes. Have a class discussion on whether the documentary depicted the LGBT community in a positive or negative way. In addition, delve more into the idea that at that time, being a homosexual was considered a mental disease according to the American Psychiatric Association.
- In 1969, the Stonewall Riots took place in New York City. Have a debate about why the riots happened. Students need to explore the perception of society at that time and be prepared to argue for or against the riots.
- In 1972, the first gay synagogue opened in the United States. Explore the significance of a religious-based organization accepting the LGBT community.
- In 1973, the American Psychiatric Association removed homosexuality from its list of mental disorders. Debate the significance of this event and whether there are people in society who believe it is a mental disease or not.
- Debate the concept that you are born a homosexual versus whether it is a choice or not.
- In 1977, Anita Bryant created a "Save our Children" campaign. Discuss the campaign and whether it was harmful or hurtful to the LGBT community. Discuss in-depth the ramifications of an antigay campaign where children are at risk of being exposed to homosexuals.
- Discuss whether the media help or hurt the LGBT community. Was there a smear campaign early on to depict homosexuals as pedophiles? In commercials, documentaries, and television shows in the 1960s, 1970s, and 1980s how were homosexuals depicted?
- What was the significance of the assassination of Harvey Milk? How did it affect the LGBT community? Watch the movie *Milk* starring Sean Penn.
- In the 1980s, the AIDS epidemic really hit the United States hard. Discuss the lasting effects of AIDS to the LGBT community. Discuss the public perception of the disease. Discuss the role the government played in helping or hurting the AIDS epidemic in the 1980s.
- Have a debate about "don't ask, don't tell." Does it hurt the military? Why was this policy created in the first place? Why was there opposition to ending the policy?

- Debate the Defense of Marriage Act that passed through Congress in 1996.
- Have a class debate about legalizing marriage. Is marriage supposed to be between a man and a woman? Why is this such an important debate? Why do you think people are not happy with the term *civil union*? Why is there a strong opposition for gays not to be allowed to be married?

Social studies is a great curricular area to incorporate discussions about LGBT issues. The public school system is a microcosm for society at large, and the students who enter school bring diverse opinions with them. The opinions generated in classroom discussions about LGBT issues do not have to be politically correct, but students do have to be respectful of one another regardless if they agree or disagree. It would be very important for teachers to set parameters for the discussions and debates, much like they do for other controversial areas.

ART, MUSIC, AND THE LGBT COMMUNITY

- Have students do an artist study and include at least one gay artist. Students can explore the life of the artist, which would include their personal life, which always shapes the artist's perspective. Andy Warhol is a good example of a gay artist.
- Have students look at photographs of the LGBT community that have been used in newspapers. Whether the photos are from Gay Pride Parades or marriage equality rallies, students can get a sense of what the artist or photographer was trying to convey in the picture.
- Look at the art of Keith Haring, who became enormously popular during the AIDS epidemic, to see what he was trying to convey in his art.
- Using art from Greek and Roman periods and exploring the nature of what the artist was painting is important to both history and art. Some of the art from that period was considered controversial, and a teacher could explore the reasons why it was considered controversial.
- In music class, include discussions of modern music and the meaning the artists are trying to convey. Singers like the Indigo Girls, Melissa Etheridge, and Lady Gaga all have songs that talk about acceptance of the LGBT community.
- Discussions about composers who were famous members of the LGBT community.
- Discussions about Broadway shows, such as *The Invention of Love*, which was the story of poet A. E. Housman and his secret love for his college roommate.

GUEST SPEAKERS WHO ADDRESS BULLYING

Did you ever notice that it is easier for a person to come from outside your school district to deliver a controversial message? Why does our staff listen to the message of a guest with more ease than a message we deliver to them? There is an old saying that you "cannot be a prophet in your own town." Perhaps guest speakers can embellish more than someone who works within the district, or they can call people out without the fear of retribution; however, whatever the reason, guest speakers can deliver our most important messages to staff.

Guest speakers can discuss bullying, and if it is someone who has been bullied themselves, or had a child who was bullied, the message can be very powerful. Most school districts and towns have nonprofit organizations fairly close by that offer these services. If your town has an LGBT Community Center or a Pride Center, those groups can offer to come in and speak to staff. Whether it is discussing the acceptance of LGBT students or antibullying campaigns, guest speakers can get to the heart of an issue.

AFTER-SCHOOL ENRICHMENT

The drama club could focus on a gay-themed play such as the *Laramie Project*. Although drama class is an elective taken by a small number of students, a play can be seen by the whole school community as well as parents in the community. Just like gay characters seen in mainstream media, a school play that has gay characters can act as a great educational tool for those who attend a play.

Extracurricular activities, other than gay–straight alliance meetings, are another important resource for LGBT students. Schools often have dances, and more importantly a prom. Allowing same-sex couples to attend these dances and the prom together can help create a climate of acceptance. After-school activities can have just as important of an impact with students as all of the things that happen during a school day. Opportunities for LGBT students that can be provided during the school day and after school can help create a positive school climate.

CONCLUSION

Adding LGBT curriculum to a school day takes bravery. The repercussions are big but so is the spreading of ignorance. By not including LGBT topics into classroom discussions, school staff also teach the hidden curriculum to LGBT youth that they are not as important as their heterosexual peers. In addition, they are sending a message to bullies and other students that ignorance is not only tolerated, but that it's taught on a daily basis. Whether it is formal curriculum such as social studies, art, or English Language Arts, or informal curriculum such as class discussions about the saying, "That's so gay," schools can have an impact on the daily lives of all students, regardless of whether they are gay or straight.

Action Steps

- Find subject area that you are comfortable with to implement in your classroom. That subject matter could be one book or a discussion about a current event.
- Have students brainstorm a list of acceptable and nonacceptable billboards or advertisements that they see in their community.
- Offer LGBT-themed books within your classroom or library.
- Hang up a picture or sticker in your classroom that symbolizes a safe space for LGBT students.
- Discuss the reasons why books get banned with your students.
- Encourage diverse, thought-provoking ways of thinking in your classroom. Encourage students to step out of their comfort zone.
- Anything can be taught to students as long as it is done in an age-appropriate way.

Discussion Questions

- Out of all the images that you see as you travel, how many depict a heterosexual lifestyle?
- How many have you seen that depict a homosexual lifestyle?
- Of the two, which one do you feel would cause the most upset in your community?
- Take the story about In Our Own Voices and relate it to the public school classroom. How many teachers would feel strong enough to take on the subject of homosexuality given the fact that many parents may complain?

(Continued)

(Continued)

- How many administrators would support those teachers that do take on the topic?
- Is the importance of integrating the subject into instruction worth the stress teachers would get from dealing with a small group of parents?
- What literature could you incorporate into your classroom that would provide exposure to LGBT issues?
- How often have you chosen not to cover a subject because you were concerned about the backlash you may receive from an administrator, colleague, or parent?
- What are the roadblocks in your school community that prevent you from offering LGBT curriculum to students?
- How can you create a change in the mindset of your students toward the LGBT community in your classroom?
- Do you believe that students are more tolerable of human variances than teachers?
- How would your colleagues react to LGBT curriculum?
- Would you advocate the teaching of LGBT curriculum in your school? Why or why not?

CHAPTER FIVE

Gay–Straight Alliances

It's interesting because there seems to be a lot of effort put into stopping gay–straight alliances from meeting, but it's a net positive for the whole school environment if you have one in place.

—Eliza Byard (DeWitt, 2011, p. 13)

Lesbian, gay, bisexual, and transgender (LGBT) students have siblings, relatives, and friends, all of whom have to come to grips with knowing their loved one is gay. When people come out, regardless of their age, those close to them sometimes feel as if they never knew their friend at all. Being in the closet is often equated to living a lie. Unfortunately, it's not living a lie as much as it is not being able to accept who you are, and not knowing if others will still love you. It also makes it difficult when adults say it is a choice or a preference. No matter what the circumstances are when someone comes out, they need a place to turn, and gay–straight alliances can be the sanctuary that LGBT students can rely on. A GSA can also be the place where their straight peers can turn to get a better understanding of LGBT issues. The reciprocal benefit is that the LGBT students can get a better understanding of their straight peers and what their misperceptions of the LGBT community might be. In addition, those straight peers can be ambassadors of change for a school climate.

Symbol of Change

It is June. Students are filled with excitement as we are in the final days of school and summer is within their reach. The bells rings; another day of school is complete, and the halls fill with students and faculty who have worked together to learn, grow, and achieve academic success. As you glance down the hall, you see two handsome young men holding hands. No one is surprised; no comments are made. The couple continues to walk hand in hand, sharing details about their day smiling, laughing, and feeling safe. They are accepted and valued. They are free to be who they are and safe to express their connection to each other.

We see heterosexual couples holding hands all of the time and generally pay no special attention to them. But holding hands is a symbol. It is a symbol of comfort; it is a symbol of connection and a symbol of pride. The young men holding hands down the hall of this high school is a symbol of acceptance, compassion, and our growth as a school community.

When students walk the halls of South Side High School, they are greeted by images that promote tolerance. Whether it is an antibullying public service announcement on our morning news program or a poster campaign that encourages respect and acceptance, our students are reminded of our commitment and mission to ensure the comfort and safety of all students.

Perhaps the young men in the hall found courage in the "safe space" stickers that are posted on our classroom doors or by the GSA showcase that is displayed proudly in our main hallway. Perhaps they found courage from attending an afterschool discussion circle hosted by the GSA on an issue that affects LGBT life.

Holding hands is a symbol. Their courage is a symbol; a symbol of our effort and growth as a school community. Since my employment began at South Side High School 8 years ago, I have seen our school evolve. I have witnessed the increased acceptance of our LGBT. I have seen first-hand random acts of kindness and compassion and a commitment to understanding that makes me proud.

Our school administration and exceptional faculty have been instrumental to these changes. Their actions and kindness help to create a climate that fosters unity and strength. Our GSA is a strong school organization that is well-supported and one that provides education and resources to the SSHS community. Through student and staff collaboration, we work diligently to uphold our mission:

To raise awareness regarding issues related to sexual identity and orientation. Through group discussions, meetings, and special events, the GSA explores the correlation between homophobia and other such oppressions. The GSA strives to ensure equal treatment of all youth and a school environment free of homophobia.

The GSA holds weekly meetings, plans school events, and campaigns and maintains a website on the district home page.

Creating a school environment that fosters both the educational, social, and emotional health of its students is essential to helping LGBT students feel empowered and truly accepted. It aids them in developing a positive self-image and gives them the strength to pursue their goals and to live their lives as their true authentic selves.

Holding hands has meaning. Holding hands is a symbol. Two young men holding hands in our hallway is a symbol of how far we have come.

—Nicole Franchesca Knorr, LCSW

"One of the most visible manifestations of the contemporary movement for social justice is in the emergence of Gay–Straight Alliances (GSA) across the United States" (Russell, Muraco, Subramaniam, & Laub, 2009, p. 892). GSAs involve students who identify as LGBT and straight students. These students find a supportive environment that helps open up a conversation about what it means to be gay in school where they are in the minority. In addition, it creates a conversation about learning to accept people who are different than one another. In more and more states, schools are offering GSAs to support LGBT students.

In a study of 1,700 students in Massachusetts, Szalacha found that "more than 50% of the public school systems in Massachusetts have GSAs" (2001, p. 11). In addition, Szalacha (2003) states, "In schools that have GSAs, students and school personnel report more supportive climates for LGBT students" (p. 69). Most likely if you have a school that is accepting enough to allow a GSA, that school has a supportive environment. A school that does not allow a GSA is most likely a more hostile environment where differences are not tolerated. Lipkin (1995) believes schools need to take a stronger stance in addition to having a GSA.

If schools are going to have an impact on the attitudes and behaviors of their sexually concerned and often active students, they must acknowledge in their curricula the importance of sexuality in our lives and in the lives of those who have gone before us. (Lipkin, 1995, p. 32)

A GSA offers an ally to LGBT students so they feel welcomed in the school where they attend, which is the same thing schools strive to offer to their straight peers every day. Because of the Equal Access Act of 1984, GSAs can be formed based on student need.

Officials need not endorse any particular student organization, but federal law requires that they afford all student groups the same opportunities to form, to convene on school grounds, and to have access to the same resources available to other student groups. (Duncan, 2011, p. 2)

If a school receives federal aid and they allow noncurriculum groups to meet outside of the school day, they must allow other non-curriculum groups to be formed as well, and GSAs are an example of a noncurriculum group. Many times students and staff do not know about the Equal Access Act and do not advocate enough to form a GSA.

HOW TO START A GSA IN YOUR SCHOOL

- Contact your principal about starting a GSA. Because of the Equal Access Act of 1984, schools must allow a GSA if there is a student need.
- Encourage students to contact the principal if they want a GSA.
- Find a class advisor (teacher, counselor, etc.) who will support a GSA. If the advisor happens to be openly gay, he may want to have a straight co-advisor. Too often when an openly gay teacher supports a "gay-themed" event, he is seen as pushing a gay agenda.
- Meet once a month. Be aware that there will be push back by the school community. Push back often comes with ideas that make others uncomfortable.
- Administrators should allow their GSA a bulletin board space if they allow spaces for other after-school groups.

WHY SCHOOLS SHOULD OFFER A GSA

In spite of the positive effect these groups can have in schools, some such groups have been unlawfully excluded from school grounds, prevented from forming, or denied access to school resources. These same barriers have sometimes been used to target religious and other student groups, leading Congress to pass the Equal Access Act (Duncan, 2011, p. 1).

Most schools in North America have sports teams. Those teams practice together 6 out of 7 days a week so they can perform better at competitions. Many students like to be a part of a team because they feel they are a part of something larger than themselves. Coaches have great influence on their athletes, and students strive to do better so they can make their coach proud. Sports fit a niche for many students and can have life-changing effects.

Besides sports, schools offer afterschool activities like drama where students can perform in plays, which provide them with an outlet for their dramatic or artistic side. Just like with sports, we know that most of these students perform better in school. Participating in an afterschool activity can help them become well-rounded, which can increase their likelihood of getting accepted to the college of their choice. In addition, it can also have life-changing effects. All students need an outlet to properly deal with their emotions, strengths, and weaknesses.

The reality is that most schools offer extra activities to students so they can flourish and become better human beings. One of the main reasons why schools exist is to prepare students for the future. If schools do this for so many of the populations of students that enter their doors, why is it that many of these schools that offer student choices do not offer GSAs? The answer is fairly simple. Most staff are afraid of the community pressure and do not want the stress. Even in the most liberal and accepting communities, there are conservative or homophobic community members who do not want their children exposed to LGBT issues. There are school officials and staff who do not think it's important to discuss LGBT issues, and they prefer a "don't ask, don't tell" policy. If schools happen to be located in a highly conservative or homophobic area, they are less likely to offer a GSA.

> Although these groups have been around for more than 20 years, students attempting to create gay–straight alliances still face many hurdles. In Clovis, New Mexico, this year, the school board voted to ban clubs that didn't have a tie to schoolwork from meeting during the day, though their sights were set on one club in particular: a gay–straight alliance Clovis High School students wanted to form. In May, the school board relented, in part because of the threat of a lawsuit from the New Mexico chapter of the American Civil Liberties Union. (Shah, 2011, n.p.)

Unfortunately, those are the areas of the country that desperately need a GSA because LGBT students who live there may be more likely to hear homophobic comments and feel very alone. "Gay–straight alliances (GSAs) and similar student-initiated groups addressing LGBT issues can play an important role in promoting safer schools and creating more welcoming learning environments" (Duncan, 2011, p. 1).

Getting someone to take on the role as an advisor for a GSA is complicated. It's common for a GSA club to look for a gay teacher because she understands the issues these students face and should want to take on the role. Unfortunately, that teacher may have concerns that she will be viewed as pushing the "gay agenda." All people have an agenda when they decide to take on a role in the public school system, which is why they are interested in being a part of the group they try to lead. It may be because they have a passion in that area or believe things need to change. Unfortunately, the use of the term "gay agenda" has negative connotations, and people try to step away from it.

In talking with several male gay teachers who took on the role of the GSA advisor, they stated that they asked a straight female teacher to co-advise with them so they did not open themselves up to too much scrutiny. If a GSA looks for a straight advisor, it usually involves a female teacher to take on the role because male straight teachers do not want to be considered gay. It takes a very secure straight male to step up to being the advisor of a GSA, but it does happen. Typically a GSA advisor has some sort of connection to the LGBT community, such as a gay relative or friend.

GSAs offer so much more than just a place for a LGBT student to belong, although that alone is highly important. Studies show that a school with a GSA has a more accepting climate, where students feel safe (Kosciw, 2007). GSAs also offer a place where straight students can come to learn about LGBT issues. In addition, if there are straight students with a gay sibling or relative, a GSA can offer a place where they can come and get a better understanding of their loved one. If a student is questioning their sexual orientation, a GSA is a great place to go and find resources that can help them in the process.

Although the efforts of these groups focus primarily on the needs of LGBT students, students who have LGBT family members and friends, and students who are perceived to be LGBT, messages of respect, tolerance, and inclusion benefit all our students. By encouraging dialogue and providing supportive resources, these groups can help make schools safe and affirming environments for everyone. (Duncan, 2011, p. 1)

Overall, GSAs are a win-win for a school system. It's a win for school administrators because it helps create a more inclusive high school where everyone feels they belong, which helps to create a more accepting school climate. It helps teachers and staff because it enriches the conversations they can have with students during class, which provides a deeper educational experience. Most importantly, it helps the students, whether they are gay or straight, because it creates a community of learners that can help educate the whole child, which makes for a better society.

THE PARAMETERS OF CREATING A GSA

"By allowing students to discuss difficult issues openly and honestly, in a civil manner, our schools become forums for combating ignorance, bigotry, hatred, and discrimination" (Duncan, 2011, p. 2).

In 2007, GLSEN published a jump-start guide for students and faculty who would like to start a GSA in their school. The guide, which can be downloaded by visiting the GLSEN website at www .GLSEN.org, describes four types of school climate. The four climates a school can have are hostile, resistant, passive, and inclusive (GLSEN, 2010, pp. 36–39). The following are examples of the four climates that schools can have. The names are fictitious, but the climates set for LGBT students are real.

Vignette ───────────────────────────────

Hostile School

Forest High School is located in a middle class suburban town in the Midwest that is considered conservative. It has a student population of 1,200 9th to 12th graders and is predominately white, with about 10% of its population being racially diverse. The words "gay" and "faggot" are commonly used by students, and teachers and staff not only ignore the name calling, but they are amused by it. Rainbow flags are used as punch lines and not as symbols of acceptance.

(Continued)

(Continued)

A senior boy named Randy is openly gay because he does not see the sense in hiding who he is, but he is scared to go to school on a daily basis. He came out to his parents his junior year, and they were shocked, saddened, angry, and went through a whole host of emotions, all in an attempt to get him to change his mind about his "sexual preference." They were embarrassed that their son was gay, and despite many attempts, they could not get him to admit it was just a phase he was going through. When he began to dye his hair and out himself to his friends, his parents couldn't take the stress so they kicked him out. He moved in with his aunt on the other side of town. His aunt is someone who prefers to go against the grain, and she is quite proud of her nephew for being who he is at such a young age. Randy dreams of the day that he graduates so that he can leave town and never come back.

As Randy walks down the hall, other boys call him a homo and the girls around him laugh at the name-calling. The friends he does have do not fit in either for a variety of reasons, so they get together on weekends and drink and talk about how great life will be when they leave. Randy has been beaten up twice in his physical education class and the teacher turned a "blind eye" to the event. Although Randy and his aunt complained to the principal, nothing was done because "no one" saw anything. In addition, the high school lacks an antibullying policy, especially where sexual orientation is concerned. The school district as a whole does not have an antibullying policy that includes sexual orientation, and no one in the school's history has ever broached the topic.

Randy became so brazen after numerous name-calling episodes that he went to the principal to ask to start a Gay–Straight Alliance. The principal, Mr. Henry, laughed and said that would never be allowed while he was principal. He then shut the door and told Randy he should tone it down a bit so he didn't get beaten up anymore. Randy knew there were a few more students who could possibly be gay. Those students, however, were too frightened to have the conversation about a GSA, and they asked him to stop pushing the envelope so much because they were afraid people would actively seek them out and abuse them as much as they abused Randy.

One afternoon Randy went to the mailbox to get his aunt's mail, and there was a paper inside with Randy's picture that had the words "faggot" and "homo" written all over it. Later that night Randy went to his computer to check his e-mail, and he received an e-mail from an anonymous person who attached the same picture with the derogatory words, and it said, "Watch your back." When Randy approached Mr. Henry, the principal said there was nothing he could do about it because it all happened off school grounds.

Randy knew his time at the hostile school was coming to a close, but he worried about all of the other LGBT students that hid because they did not feel safe. He wondered how many would drop out of school or move to another town. He also knew that most staff at Forest High School couldn't *care less that LGBT students moved because it just meant that they would no longer be at their high school. He spent most days during his senior year wishing they were different. Wishing that he went to a more open and accepting high school.*

Although the example of the hostile high school is fictitious, the story is real and you need only to read newspapers to see stories about LGBT students who are abused or who die by suicide because they do not attend high schools that are open and accepting. The reality is that hostile schools contribute to the hatred of LGBT students in North America because they do not have policies in place and ignore the abuse the students face on a daily basis.

Vignette

The Resistant School

Taylor High School is located in a lower middle class rural town in the South that is considered moderately conservative. It has a student population of 800 9th to 12th graders and is relatively racially diverse, with about 35% of its population being African American, 15% Latino, and 50% white. The words "gay" and "faggot" are commonly used by students, but some teachers and staff address it when they hear the words used. Most staff members, however, condone the use of the language because they believe it's a case of "kids being kids."

Several students are openly gay because they feel it is important to be who they are, even if it makes others a bit uncomfortable. They also feel that they can change the climate of their school by being out and hope to one day have a GSA. The principal, knowing the Equal Access Act, has allowed the organization of the club with the stipulation that they need a faculty advisor, but none of the teachers or staff has expressed an interest. In addition, the LGBT students would like to see some books on the topic in the library or have some debates about LGBT issues in social studies, but so far that has not happened. However, health class covers LGBT curriculum, but it is confined to information about HIV/AIDS.

Emily plays lacrosse, does well in school, and has been struggling with her sexual identity. Although she thinks her parents would be supportive if she came out, she has not said anything to anyone because she does not feel comfortable with how people may react. She is constantly surrounded with heterosexual images in school and hears other girls in the locker room spreading rumors about some of the gay guys in school.

(Continued)

(Continued)

One day, a debate in social studies class erupted after hearing a news story about same-sex marriage, and Emily found herself overly concerned that people were staring at her even though she did not bring up the topic. No other LGBT students were in class at the time. Many of Emily's classmates talked about how it was morally wrong to allow same-sex couples to get married. The teacher agreed with the sentiment. The following day, the teacher announced she would not be discussing any more "gay" issues because too many parents complained that the school was trying to push a homosexual agenda. Emily knew that was not true because the school was as homophobic as the parents who complained.

Resistant schools are one step away from being hostile, but they do allow LGBT conversations to take place and have an open and out population of LGBT students. Unfortunately, those students do not feel safe and accepted in the school community. Teachers, school psychologists, and staff members are open and accepting of LGBT students, but they would prefer that gay and lesbian students not make their status so open to others.

Most schools fall between resistant and passive. A passive school has a level of acceptance greater than the resistant school, but they still have a great deal of work to do when it comes to keeping LGBT students safe. A passive school is a microcosm of society at large because the attributes are the same. The following vignette is a fictitious example of a passive high school.

Vignette

Passive School

Wilkins High School is located in a middle class town in the north that is considered moderately liberal. It has a student population of 1,500 9th to 12th graders and is relatively racially diverse, with about 15% of its population being African American, 15% Latino, 15% Asian, and 55% white. The words "gay" and "faggot" are not commonly used by students, but when they are used in the hallway by students, most teachers and staff address it.

Numerous students are openly gay because they feel safe, and they formed a GSA about 6 years ago. The principal has allowed the organization of the club with the stipulation that they need a faculty advisor and a male teacher who is openly gay co-advises the GSA with a heterosexual female teacher. The library has a section of books dedicated to LGBT students, and a few teachers bring up debates that involve the LGBT community. One of the three Health teachers includes the LGBT community in the conversations about abstinence.

The Wilkins GSA has been allowed to have one bulletin board across from the classroom where they meet. The bulletin board has been vandalized a few times by students who write derogatory statements that include the words "faggot" and "queer." One time the student who vandalized the bulletin board was caught and suspended by the principal because the school has a new student code of conduct that includes sexual orientation. The school district also includes a board policy that includes sexual orientation language as well.

Although Wilkins High School seems progressive, it still has work to do because there are some staff members who will not address the harassment of students based on sexual orientation. In addition, although some teachers discuss LGBT topics in the classroom, most of the staff will not because they do not believe there is a place for it.

The GSA has a 3-year plan that includes the initiative to provide more exposure to the student population about LGBT issues.

Most schools strive to be the Passive School that is described above, and most LGBT students would love to attend a school like the fictitious Wilkins High School. A school where all students are safe and LGBT students feel that they can express who they are is important, and Wilkins High School would provide that opportunity to students.

The most progressive school that GLSEN (2007) refers to in its startup guide is called the Inclusive School. Although GLSEN does not provide examples of real schools that have an inclusive environment, there are schools like it that exist. The following vignette is my interpretation of an inclusive school.

Vignette

The Inclusive School

Westside High School is located in a middle class town in Long Island, New York, and is considered liberal. It has a student population of 1,350 9th to 12th graders and is relatively racially diverse, with about 20% of its population being African American, 17% Latino, 20% Asian, and 43% white. The words "gay" and "faggot" are not allowed to be used by students, and most students know that the words are derogatory and would not use them.

Numerous students are openly gay because they feel safe, and they formed a GSA about 15 years ago. The faculty advisors are two female teachers. One is openly gay and the other is heterosexual, which provides a good mix of both heterosexual and homosexual conversations. In addition, one

(Continued)

(Continued)

male teacher attends GSA meetings when he is not doing his duties as an assistant coach with the high school football team. The GSA has one bulletin board across from the classroom where they meet, but they also offer public service announcements on the morning news in school.

The library has a section of books dedicated to LGBT students, and the librarian also offers examples of how LGBT topics can be embedded in the curriculum. She also sends out e-mail blasts announcing LGBT issues, just like she does with issues of other diverse groups. In addition, all teachers initiate debates that involve the LGBT community. At one recent high school assembly, the Debate Club disputed the recent "don't ask, don't tell" policy that was repealed. Although not all students were in support of the repeal of "don't ask, don't tell," they were taught how to disagree respectfully. Both Health teachers include the LGBT community in their conversations about abstinence, and the English Language Arts teachers include LGBT literature and author studies in their curriculum.

Westside High School offers parent outreach for parents who are dealing with the emotion of having a child come out, and they work with the local LGBT Community Center to provide professional development for teachers and staff so they can best meet the needs of their LGBT student population. They have had several guest speakers come to address LGBT issues because every January the school offers a speaker's forum. The forums range from educational topics for teachers and staff to sessions that help with parenting (applying for college, dealing with teenagers, etc.).

Westside High School has a progressive code of conduct that has inclusive language for LGBT students. In addition, the school district has a strict antibullying policy that prohibits bullying based on gender and sexual orientation, among other attributes that students use to bully others. However, the school district does not have an issue with bullying because students have learned to respect one another no matter how diverse they may be.

An Inclusive School is based on the premise that all students, no matter their size, color, gender, or sexual orientation, deserve to come to school and feel safe when they arrive there.

EVENTS HELD BY A GSA

A GSA should have the mission to expose all students, staff, and teachers to the issues that LGBT students face when they enter school or when they go home to their community. There are many different ways that GSAs can educate their school community. One of the most important ways is by having a group in the first place.

Schools with GSAs have less bullying and a safer school climate. In addition, they send the message to the whole school and community that LGBT students deserve to have a voice.

Schools can support GSAs by providing them with a link on their school website. Many GSAs are allowed to meet at schools, but many are not given a page on school websites, which almost seems like a "don't ask, don't tell" policy, especially if other clubs are allowed a space on the school website. The GSA link can offer information for students and parents as well as educate the school community of events taking place.

One major event that GSAs should plan every year is the No Name Calling Week, which is sponsored by GLSEN. No Name Calling Week tells all students that using phrases like "that's so gay" is not appropriate. In addition, a GSA can sponsor the Safe Space Campaign, which is also sponsored by GLSEN. The Safe Space Campaign provides schools with a kit, and within the kit are educational material and rainbow-colored triangles that symbolize a safe space for LGBT students and other students who are feeling threatened for their gender expression.

Quality GSAs should also offer public service announcements for students on the morning announcements. Whether it's a promotion of the above events or an announcement about Gay Pride, which happens in June every year, an announcement on the part of a GSA can offer valuable information. GSAs can also sponsor dances as well as other school events and offer information tables where they can provide educational materials to all students regarding LGBT issues. A GSA is a valuable resource and should be seen in every high school, regardless of the community the school is in.

CONCLUSION

Unfortunately, a very small number of schools offer GSAs to LGBT and heterosexual students. Research shows that GSAs can help keep students engaged in school and help create a more open and accepting school climate, but unfortunately it also opens schools up to the risk of losing community support and creating community tension.

GSAs are worth the risk that they may expose schools to because those students involved will feel as if they are a part of something. Creating a GSA may be difficult at the beginning, but over time it will become an accepted part of the school community. It will be worth all the hard work when a GSA is as much as an institution as sports and arts programs are at a school. The first step in creating a GSA is to make sure that a school district has the appropriate policies in place. The importance of school codes of conduct and school board policies will be explored in the following chapter.

Action Steps

- Talk to staff members you trust to see if they would support a GSA.
- Every school has outspoken students who have a passion for civil rights. Talk with them about school climate, and see if they would be interested in starting a GSA.
- GSAs need both straight and gay members, so encourage all students who are interested to join. A mixed group means that they will be able to have a stronger voice for the GSA.
- A GSA should have a bulletin board space in the school hallway. Unfortunately, there is a potential that other students will vandalize that space. Don't let that stop you.
- Contact other schools that have GSAs. Go to www.gsanetwork.org for more information about establishing a GSA.
- If you receive push back, please refer to the Equal Access Act of 1984. That allows you to establish a GSA.
- If you are an administrator, as much as you may come under scrutiny for allowing a GSA, it is worth it to your school community.
- If your school district has a board policy regarding harassment and discrimination because of sexual orientation and gender expression, this should help you in your quest to establish a GSA.

Discussion Questions

- How would your community react to a GSA in your school?
- Is your school administrator supportive of a GSA?
- Why is it important to have a GSA in your school setting?
- What are the positive aspects of allowing a GSA?
- What are the negative aspects of allowing a GSA?
- What is the first step you could take to organize a GSA in your school?
- What outside groups could you contact to support you in establishing a GSA?
- What is the first event you could plan with your GSA?

CHAPTER SIX

Following Through

School Board Policies and Codes of Conduct

Youth suicides prompted by anti-gay bullying have brought unprecedented public attention to LGBT school safety. And while we need to make sure every individual student is safe, a decade of research shows that the problem of discrimination and harassment in schools needs to be addressed through policy. It is time to focus on state laws and school and district policies that can make our schools safer for all children. (Russell, 2011, p. 25)

School administrators understand that power and influence with parents and students increase when their school district has a school board policy to support them. However, most policies that protect students from harassment and bullying include language about gender and ethnicity but do not include language regarding sexual orientation or gender expression. One such state law that will change that is the Dignity for All Students Act, which was passed in New York state in June of 2010 and will go into effect on July 1, 2012. It stipulates that all public schools in New York state need to have board policies that include language regarding sexual orientation and gender expression, among many other areas. Washington state has adopted a policy requiring schools to include the same language as New York state, and many other states are following their lead. All states should, and hopefully will, follow this important legislation.

Washington State Takes Steps to Protect LGBTQ Students

The department of education in Washington state, called the Office of Superintendent of Public Instruction (OSPI), follows state statute in address-ing the needs of our LGBTQ [lesbian, gay, bisexual, transgender, question-ing] students. We are fortunate that our legislators have chosen to protect Washington's K–12 students from harassment, intimidation, and bullying (HIB) based on sexual orientation, gender identity, and gender expression. In our work with school districts, OSPI attempts to bring to the surface the protection that has been granted all Washington students. We do this in the following ways:

We name the protected groups at every opportunity, so that LGBTQ students and families know that students are granted protection by state law from harassment, intimidation, and bullying.

- *Our State HIB Policy and State HIB Procedure, which all 295 school districts must adopt, names sexual orientation, gender expression, and gender identity as three classes that are protected from harassment, intimidation, or bullying. The policy must be shared widely with stu-dents, staff, and families on a public site.*
- *Our guidance document, HIB Policy and Procedure Frequently Asked Questions, makes clear that districts must name sexual orientation, gender identity, and gender expression in policy and procedure. It also provides districts with flexibility if they believe outing a student to their families could bring harm to the student at home (see below).*
  - *"Does the HIB policy give special protections to any group?"*
  - *"No. You will notice, however, that the policy and procedure call out certain groups that are known to experience HIB at a greater rate than the general population. These groups need to be named—and protected—in district policy and procedure. Under a different law— RCW 28A.642—some students are given special protections against discrimination based on race, color, religion, ancestry, national origin, gender, sexual orientation, including gender expression or identity, and mental or physical disability."*
  - *"The procedure says that in rare cases, if a district has evidence that contacting a parent may threaten the health and safety of a student, the district may choose not to notify a parent that their child is being bullied. Don't parents always have the right to know what's happening with their child?"*
- *"A district's first choice is always to work with families when a student is in trouble. There are rare exceptions, though, where a school has determined that a student may be severely harmed as a result of a parent/guardian receiving information about a child. That's one of the reasons why in Washington state youth—typically youth 13 and older—can receive STD services, HIV testing, alcohol and drug treatment, contraceptives, prenatal care, and other services*

without the notification of a parent. In cases where a district, after consultation with a psychologist, counselor, or social worker, believes it is not in a student's best interest to involve a parent/guardian initially, they may be able to find opportunities to involve families later in the process."

We have built a School Safety Center webpage, called Lesbian, Gay, Bisexual, Transgender, Questioning (LGBTQ) Youth, expressly for the LGBTQ population. Our LGBTQ page identifies the state documents that provide them with protection from harassment, intimidation, and bullying; we explain, using national data, why sexual minority youth need special protection; we provide them with links to Federal sites, including the CDC [Centers for Disease Control and Prevention] and Department of Education LGBTQ sites, that provide updated resources and support; we include a popular culture site, called the It Gets Better Campaign, that lets LGBTQ students know LGBTQ youth grow up to be successful adults; we include a piece on making schools welcoming to straight students that have same-sex parents; and we include Washington state sites that have broad appeal and can provide local support.

We created a webpage for students in crisis, called SOS for Youth, which gives students confidential and immediate access to helplines. We've included contact information for Washington's Safe Schools Coalition, the Trevor Project, and the Gay, Lesbian, Straight, Education Network (GLSEN).

For additional information contact Jeff Soder, Ph.D., Supervisor, Office of Superintendent of Public Instruction, Olympia, WA, jeff.soder@k12.wa.us 360-725-6044.

McLaren says that "we rely as a society on perceptions that have been filtered through constellations of historical commentaries rooted in xenophobia, homophobia, racism, sexism, the commodification of everyday life, and the reproduction of race, class and gender relations" (1995, p. 105). Just like the media focus on the stereotypes of LGBT individuals, McLaren stated that schools do these things as well. "Schools both mirror and motivate such perceptions, reproducing a culture of fear that contributes to a wider justification for vigilance surrounding sexual practices through polar definitions of youth as morally upright/sexually deviant, and approvingly decent/unrepentantly corrupt" (1995, p. 106).

Some very progressive schools want to create a safe and nurturing atmosphere for all students, including those who are gay and lesbian. Szalacha asserts that "educators are coming to believe that they have a social responsibility to provide an environment that both supports the ability of all students—including lesbians and gays to learn and is free from physical and psychological abuse" (2001, p. 8). As New York state and Washington state moves into a direction to make sure that administrators have the school board policies they need to support them as they confront this issue, there is still a concern that the staff will not address name calling and bullying in the hallways when the administrators are not around, regardless of whether professional development has been offered.

Vignette

Nirvana?

After 5 years of being an Assistant Principal at Averill Park High School, there is no question that I have landed in a unique place with regards to the status of GLBT students within the school's culture. From my first week on the job the Superintendent, an openly gay woman herself, often called it "Nirvana." Still, the things I have witnessed within the walls of my building never cease to amaze me, and they often make me smile. What is more baffling is the question of how a tremendously homogeneous, rural community such as ours has managed to create a school environment that is safer and more accepting than so many others throughout the nation.

It would be easy to give a great deal of credit to the fact that our Code of Conduct and Board policies are well-designed, annually reviewed, and inclusive documents that specifically identify "sexual orientation" as a protected group. This, however, is far too simple and doesn't reflect the real work that makes our success so tangible. In the relatively short time that I have been a school administrator, I have certainly learned that any policy is only as good as the day-to-day practice behind it. This isn't to say that having inclusive policies is not a tremendously important first step. It does, after all, reflect that the community has actually recognized the need to support and protect GLBT students in the first place! I simply feel that it is important to remember that it is a means to an end. Ultimately, policy is only a precursor to supporting the hard work that is necessary each and every day...and this takes committed people!

As my mind plays through the images that I believe most reflect the positive climate we have sustained for our GLBT students, I am aware that it has required the commitment, perseverance, and dedication of a core group of individuals, both students and adults, who have created practices that have slowly transformed our culture. Our administrative team actively addresses all forms of bullying and harassment, recognizing the need to balance punitive responses with those that are more proactive and educational in nature. Each year, we have more and more adults who are willing to "say something" when they see students, GLBT or otherwise, being targeted in our hallways, cafeteria, or their classrooms. Our long-standing GSA has strived to educate and involve everyone in our school community through the establishment of "safe spaces" throughout the building; places where students know that there is a trusted adult ally with whom they can talk. Our annual celebrations of National Coming-Out Day and the Day of Silence have brought further awareness to many throughout the school. Even as we build a new Freshman Seminar, one of the primary objectives will be to foster a sense of class identity and teach students the skills they need to become peer allies. Of course, I firmly believe that it has helped a great deal that we have so many openly gay and lesbian role models among our faculty, staff, and administration.

No matter how much positive I see each day, I am always reminded that we are engaged in an ongoing process. Like any other school, we still struggle with the fact that terms like "gay," "faggot," and "dyke" are so ubiquitously thrown around in our hallways and classrooms. There are still adults who simply don't engage in addressing harassment and bullying, perhaps out of ignorance or fear, or perhaps because they have yet to develop the skills to do so. Each year, we must respond to handfuls of e-mails and parent complaints expressing disgust over our choice to recognize National Coming-Out Day or Day of Silence. Recently, one parent stood outside of our building to hand out antigay religious flyers in protest of our practices. A rogue Board of Education member has even maintained an ongoing anonymous blog that publicly bashes and slanders the many gay and lesbian adults in our school community, both professionally and personally.

Fortunately, the voices of these few remain small in comparison to the forward movement and success we have experienced. They are, quite simply, a reality that we must continue to address. Any educator who truly cares about young people must be willing to continue to teach our students, and our communities, to treat everyone with respect no matter what others might say or do, and regardless of who someone is. Despite the sometimes contradictory bits and pieces of our school community, we continue to address, to educate, and to move forward with the patience and respect that we expect of others. This can, and must, happen with or without policy that supports such practice.

I see it each year at our Senior Dinner Dance, when several same-sex couples attend and enjoy the evening with the total acceptance of their peers. Our Junior Prom court has had many, many openly gay and lesbian students elected to it over the years, as well. Last year alone, there were three! I remember how surprised and delighted I was when, 2 years ago, the student who was elected by his class as "Mr. AP," the senior who most embodies the spirit of the class, was an openly gay young man. Each day, as I walk the halls and visit the classrooms of my school, I am always pleased to see that students, no matter who they are, can be themselves.

Our inclusive policies were merely a stepping stone to getting to these wonderful moments. I credit the ongoing and brilliant work of the many, many adults and students who, each and every day, make it a priority to insure that everyone is treated with the respect and dignity that they deserve.

—Heath Hanley
Albany, New York

Laws That Support School Decisions

Sometimes schools do not protect all students. Many schools send a very clear message that lesbian, gay, bisexual, and transgender (LGBT) students cannot or should not be "out." Other times they have an unwritten "don't ask, don't tell" policy. Gay students can be gay, but they should not bring attention to themselves or they may suffer some consequences.

A strategy used to support schools as they safeguard LGBT students is through the use of state laws. In addition to the Dignity for All Students Act in New York state Executive Law, Article 15 prohibits discrimination based on sexual orientation. Schools within New York state must comply with this law and many set policies based on it. In the event that discrimination does happen based on someone's sexual orientation, schools have the law to support any decision they make. Schools can make bold statements by highlighting these antidiscrimination and antiharassment policies yearly in school newsletters.

School Leaders Embracing the Sexual Diversity of Students

"Recognizing the existence of [LGBT] students and faculty, as well as including any sexual issues in core programs of study, can threaten the social structure of the school, especially for those who gain from that structure" (Bielaczyc, 2001, p. 9). This means that some educators and administrators have control over their social structures like the faculty, classrooms, and school buildings, and they lack the openness and acceptance for things they cannot control. Discussions around LGBT issues is one of those areas that make people feel uncomfortable, so they do what they can to not allow the discussions to take place in their classrooms.

Being supportive of programs and discussions of LGBT issues can create stress for those administrators who support them and the teachers who teach them. Many find LGBT discussions stressful because of outside influences like parents, the community, or the fear of losing their job. However, teachers need strong administrators who will support them because of those outside influences who are against the teaching of LGBT issues.

Recently in New York state, the senate approved the Same-Sex Marriage Bill, which allowed same-sex couples to get married. New York state became the sixth and largest state to allow gay marriage on June 24, 2011. As much as this was a major move forward for the LGBT community, it also brought out those people who opposed same-sex marriage, believing strongly that marriage should remain between a man and a woman. Hundreds of protestors lined the hallways of the Capital Building in Albany, New York, holding signs denouncing the right for gays to marry. Social networking sites such as Facebook lit up with comments from people who opposed same-sex marriage. Even as gay rights groups cheered New York's adoption of same-sex marriage last month, their opponents called the vote an isolated setback and started planning how to use the specter of New York to rally their troops and fill their coffers for the battles ahead.

When the media cover a story, they look at it from both sides. They interviewed same-sex opponents and same-sex supporters. Students questioning their sexual orientation or those who are closeted may be more apt to remain quiet out of fear of abuse and harassment. This type of situation should make schools more concerned about having policies in place as well as including LGBT issues into class discussions.

Cochrane states, "Alongside specifically religious institutions, lobby groups have formed to influence legislators to preserve traditional concepts of family and to regulate desire" (2004, p. 164). This has implications for school systems because they receive state and federal funding, and there is often a fear that they will be under scrutiny because of their desire to implement LGBT curriculum. However, that fear is unwarranted. Schools should be obligated to teach about sexual diversity if they do receive state funding, especially considering that they are obligated to do so under the Equal Access Act.

In the 2007 GLSEN survey of 1,580 K–12 school principals, researchers found that "three quarters of principals (75%) believe that administrators in their school would be supportive of efforts that specifically address issues of school safety for LGBT students and families" (2007, p. 12). In the same survey, "Six in ten principals (57%) believe that students would be supportive of such efforts" (Kosciw, 2007, p. 12). Bielaczyc states, "Clearly, however, the tone set by the administrator can have a great effect on the culture and attitude of the school population" (2001, p. 9). Given the results of both studies, administrators can have a powerful impact on their school's culture.

Over the past 10 years, schools have begun to see the importance of creating safe and nurturing environments for sexually diverse students. Szalacha (2001) focused her research on the Massachusetts Public School System, which is very progressive in the area of LGBT issues. Schneck (2008) researched the need to change antigay language that has been allowed to abuse gay and lesbian students for years. One of the common threads in both studies was the idea that school districts had to set policies in order to change behavior on the part of students, parents, and staff. The reason for the need to have policies in place is the fact that they are often what school boards use to support decisions they make within school systems.

"Students attending schools with an antibullying policy that included protections based on sexual orientation or gender identity/expression experienced lower levels of harassment and were more likely to report that staff intervened when hearing homophobic remarks" (GLSEN, 2009, p. 126). As important as it is for school leaders to embrace sexually diverse students so their staff feels supported, it is just as important for school boards to support students in the LGBT community. Support begins from the top down, and school administrators need to feel supported. As a school administrator, I have seen the damage one or two unsupportive board members can do to the work of even the strongest school administrator. Safeguarding LGBT students must be a shared vision.

A Shared Vision: Creating School Codes of Conduct

Schools are partnerships, in effect, between teachers, legislators, parents, and community members—all of whom already act autonomously. Thus a shared vision effort in school should begin by calling people to come together to think and act, with the power they already have, about the things that are important to them. (Senge et al., 2000, p. 291)

We need to add language regarding the safeguarding of LGBT students to codes of conduct for a variety of reasons. First, it provides administrators with the written language they need to properly discipline students who harass and bully LGBT students. Second, it sends a message to the parents who read the codes of conduct that bullying and harassment of LGBT students will not be tolerated. Third, it promotes the sense of a safe and respectful school climate because it is addressed in the code of conduct. By writing the language, administrators are addressing the issue to some extent. If it is not written in the code of conduct, it is sending a hidden message that the schools do not care about that population of students. If it is not written, then to some extent the problem remains invisible and we all know it.

It all begins with finding the right wording and having district administrators who will support building administrators. See the box on this page for one example of a student code of conduct that explains a student's rights.

STUDENTS' RIGHTS

The district is committed to safeguarding the rights given to all students under state and federal law. In addition, to promote a safe, healthy, orderly, and civil school environment, all district students have the right to:

- Treat other students with respect.
- Take part in all district activities on an equal basis regardless of race, color, creed, national original, religion, gender, or sexual orientation or disability.
- Present their version of the relevant events to school personnel authorized to impose a disciplinary penalty in connection with the imposition of the penalty.
- Access school rules and, when necessary, receive an explanation of those rules from school personnel.
- To proceed in a safe school atmosphere without the fear of threat to their well-being.

The box on this page addresses the discipline procedures that students would face if they violated the code. As important as the language is, it is equally as important to follow through with the discipline as well.

INTIMIDATION AND HARASSMENT

(Physical/emotional) intimidation, hazing, bullying, threats of harm, threatening language, assault, fighting, attempting to incite a serious incident that compromises the school environment or student safety, etc.

Use of slurs relating to ethnicity, disability, religion, race, sexual orientation, or physical condition of another, and any form of sexual harassment

Each Offense

- Investigation of complaint
- Contact parent/guardian
- 1 to 5 day(s) extended school detention (ESD) or out of school suspension, at discretion of investigating administrator. Physical injury of another student will always result in a minimum of 1 day out of school suspension.
- Superintendent's hearing, as warranted
- Police notified, as warranted
- Referral to school counselor
- Loss of parking privilege for up to 12 months

We know, as administrators, that many students and parents come into our offices and try to defend themselves by stating that they did not know they were breaking a rule or that their child did not know they were breaking a rule. By articulating exactly who is protected, administrators can defend their discipline procedures.

CREATING SCHOOL BOARD POLICIES

Creating school board policies is a more complicated issue, and one that potentially can be much more political. School board policies have to be introduced to the board of education by the school superintendent. The superintendent provides the school board with a draft of the policy that it must read prior to the school board meeting. During the school board meeting, the school board typically asks questions about the policy. Why is it needed? Why are the changes being made to the already existing policy? Do we have a bullying problem that we are not aware of? How many gay students do we really have? Being a school board member is a very political position, and therefore board members who are not agreeable to such a policy have political ways to make sure they do not have to address the issue of protecting LGBT students. They can be absent for the board meeting where these topics come up. They can abstain from the vote based on a dislike of the language used in the policy.

During the discussion, it is common for the school board to debate and change the language of the proposed policy. In addition, if a school board of education allows for public comment, the public can comment on the proposed policy. Depending on the community, public comment can be filled with discussions on both sides of the issue. Sometimes the comments may be one-sided because the community strongly believes for or against the policy. As school administrators we have seen letters from parents who believe we are overstepping our boundaries where sexual orientation is concerned. Those oppositional parents believe there is no place for discussions regarding LGBT issues in the classroom.

After the first reading of a school board policy, it is the board's right to ask for an edited version, which results in a second reading of the policy. In some cases, with less political policies, the school board accepts the policies on the first draft. School boards do not need the votes of their community to pass a school board policy. However, voting yes on a policy that a school community is not in favor of does have negative implications for the board member who votes in favor of it. As with public officials, community members feel it is their right to voice their opinions. In talking with a few school board members, it came up in conversation that they all have received hateful e-mails that community members sent them using anonymous or bogus e-mails.

It is very important for boards of education to have written policies that include language regarding LGBT students, because the board is there to protect all students. Sometimes speaking up against a close-minded community is an important step toward change.

How Parents, Staff, and Students Can Help

Grassroots efforts can have an extraordinary impact on school systems. Schools need to be a place of democracy that exposes students to all walks of life, regardless of race, religion, gender, and sexual orientation. If parents pay taxes and send their children to school to be educated, they should be able to apply pressure to schools to make sure that all groups have equal access to a quality education. They do not all have to agree, but they should have the option to participate.

Parents should contact school board members to advocate for policies that include language that specifically address LGBT issues. Parents and students may not have the right to write the school board policies that safeguard LGBT students, but they do have the right to assemble a group of taxpayers to ask for policies to be created.

CONCLUSION

Over the past few years, we have entered a time of change, and not everyone likes change, because it's uncomfortable. It's about letting go of long-time feelings in exchange for new ideas. In many cases, it may attribute to the way someone was raised, and it's tough to question that.

As much as things have changed for the better for the LGBT community, there is still a lot of negativity that surrounds them. Whether it's states that are fighting for equal rights or gay marriage, there are many opponents who do not believe the LGBT community deserves equal rights. For every proponent that says that being gay is not a choice, there are opponents that say it's a preference that can be changed.

LGBT discussions are still considered controversial at both the public school and collegiate level, which is odd because one would think a place of education would be about offering a progressive education to all students, and LGBT issues and topics would fit into that mission. However, that is not true. School systems are behind society, not in front of it. Old rules and old ways of thinking still control what teachers can teach and students can learn.

Around North America, there are great programs for LGBT students but there are clearly more needed. Too many schools and colleges lack any real supports for LGBT students. It would be beneficial if they would consider adding the following to the work they do with students on a daily basis. The following are some highlights from this book, and I would like to challenge readers to begin doing these things in their schools. To quote a LGBT youth from Rochester, "You don't have to do everything. You just have to do something."

Clearly the best way to set a climate of respect and acceptance is to make sure that issues are addressed by using proper discipline when problems arise. In addition, it is highly important to add curriculum about LGBT issues. Making sure those topics come up naturally is important, but also putting them in place by adding books and discussions is highly effective as well. Creating this kind of inclusive climate takes time, and it is hard work. Administrators, teachers, and staff need to be consistent when they are addressing LGBT issues.

The reality is that there really is no excuse for ignoring LGBT issues because that would be irresponsible on the part of the school system. Research tells us that students are coming out or questioning at a younger age. They deserve to feel safe as they enter this very stressful time in their lives. To have supports around them will keep them engaged in school and could give them a positive start for the rest of their lives. When students do not feel supported, they tend to be self-destructive and participate in behaviors that could be disastrous to their future.

In addition, we also know that we have more gay parents enrolling their children in our schools. Schools do better when they have proper parental involvement, and an inclusive school allows for parent participation on the part of gay parents. When a school is noninclusive, it is unlikely that LGBT parents will be involved in school and more likely they will support their children from home.

Throughout this book, I have tried to provide numerous ways that curriculum can be included in schools. Examples of curriculum that could be used could begin with the use of literature in English classes that focus on gay issues or books that have openly gay characters. Librarians can include LGBT literature and act as a great resource for getting books that focus on gay topics. Using literature that focuses on controversial topics is a great way to open up debate among students, which can lead to a better understanding of the issue. These debates can challenge conventional wisdom and lead students and staff to a better understanding of LGBT issues. Over the past few years, there has been a plethora of LGBT issues that have come up for debate in our society. Gay marriage, equal rights, the right to adopt, "Don't ask, don't tell," gay marriage, and Supreme Court decisions that affect the LGBT community all can lead to powerful discussions in the classroom.

Extracurricular activities, other than gay–straight alliance meetings, are another important resource for LGBT students. Schools often have dances, and more importantly a prom. Allowing same-sex couples to attend these dances and the prom together can help create a climate of acceptance.

When watching television and seeing debates about LGBT issues, it's hard to watch people speak up to say that the members of the LGBT community deserve less than their heterosexual peers. In addition, it's just as hard to hear the sympathy people have for the LGBT community because it must be so sad to be gay. LGBT community members do not want sympathy, they want equality.

Parents coming to grips with a homosexual child need someone to turn to, especially if they lack exposure to the LGBT community. I feel it is important that schools offer guidance for these parents so they have the supports they need as they become comfortable with having a gay child, even if that means referring parents to a Gay and Lesbian Community Center.

Schools need to partner with parents to make sure that all students are accepted into the school community. Hearing stories about gay students who are on court at the prom and allowed to bring their same-sex date is very exciting, but I would also venture to guess it's the exception, not the norm. Schools need to work with parents to make sure that this is more of the reality for our students, because it makes the school community much more inclusive, which means it is a place where all students can learn.

Action Steps

- Have a discussion with your administrator to find out if you have anti-harassment and antibullying policies that include language protecting sexual orientation and gender expression.
- Speak with your school superintendent about adding inclusive language to school board policies.
- Meet with school administrators to ensure that inclusive language is added to school codes of conduct.
- Make sure that newsletters that are sent home provide updates with school board policies.
- Make sure that all staff follow through on addressing behavior on the part of all students, including sexual orientation and gender expression.

Discussion Questions

- Why do you believe that school board policies do not include inclusive language that safeguards students based on sexual orientation and gender expression?
- Why do you believe it is so difficult to get that language included in codes of conduct and board policies?
- What are the advantages of having that language included in policies and codes of conduct?
- What are the disadvantages of having that language included in board policies and codes of conduct?
- How open is your community to including inclusive language in policies and codes of conduct?
- Would your board of education support such language?
- How often do you address behavior in the hallway that breaks a policy or code of conduct?
- Do you work with a supportive administrator who would advocate for this language?

Questions to Ponder

- What are the negative consequences to safeguarding LGBT students?
- What are the positive reasons for safeguarding LGBT students?
- After reading this book, do you believe that schools should create safeguards through codes of conduct and school board policies?
- Do you know any LGBT students?
  - How safe do they feel in your school?
  - Do they get called names and ignore it?
  - How are they treated by their peers?
  - How are they treated by their teachers?
  - How are they treated by their parents?
- How will you try to change your school climate?
- What is one way that you can implement safeguards for LGBT students in your school?
- Would you consider establishing a GSA?
- Would you include one book in your classroom or school library that includes an LGBT character?
- Would you place a GLSEN Safe Space sticker on your classroom or office door?

CHAPTER SEVEN

Important Stories From Higher Education

As much as we want to see inclusive high schools where students feel comfortable coming out, we know that there are still thousands of students who cannot take that important step forward. They may feel unsafe in their high school setting or even within their home environment, and sometimes may not know they are gay until they get out of their home communities.

Fortunately, there is important work being done in the college setting that may assist those students who wait until college to come out. The following vignettes are examples of college programs that help support the lesbian, gay, bisexual, and transgender (LGBT) student community. Their work offers the same important supports that all students need and hopefully works as a bridge for students who enter college after attending an unsupportive high school setting.

Vignette

LGBT Centers in Higher Education

A 2010 national study, the most comprehensive to date, surveyed 5,149 bisexual students, faculty, staff, and administrators in higher education. The results support previous research indicating that the LGBT population is the least accepted compared to other disenfranchised groups, and revealed alarming rates of anti-LGBT bias (Rankin, 2010).

(Continued)

(Continued)

- *University campus climates are frequently heterosexist and unwelcoming toward LGBT and questioning individuals.*
- *Gay, lesbian, bisexual, and queer (GLBQ) students are more than twice as likely to be harassed on campus than heterosexual and gender-conforming students.*
- *More than one third of transgender students have negative perceptions of their campuses.*
- *Approximately one third of LGBT students seriously consider leaving their institutions compared with their heterosexual peers*

With the (recent and overdue) awareness of the harassment and discrimination that LGBT students face and the negative consequences thereof—particularly with regard to academic success—university administrators are increasingly recognizing their responsibility to this population. Indeed, for many administrators, ensuring an affirming environment for LGBT students is not only a professional obligation, but also an ethical one.

But what, exactly, must administrators do to fulfill their commitment to a safe and productive educational experience for all students? In addition to the bare minimum of including gender identity/expression and sexual orientation in nondiscrimination policies and procedures, administrators must allot resources that promote the learning and development of LGBT students and their peers. Many institutions do this primarily through a dedicated department that is professionally staffed with experts in the field of student development, social justice, and gender and sexual minority issues. Modeled in many ways after multicultural centers that bring safety, support, education, and advocacy on behalf of students of color, LGBT centers serve these necessary functions on behalf of LGBT students.

Although the need is great, only about 7% of all institutes of higher education have a LGBT center/office (this works out to be approximately 200 centers nationwide) (Rankin, 2010). However, when properly staffed and accorded sufficient financial and physical resources, LGBT centers can help foster a welcoming and affirming environment in which to work and learn.

The efforts of LGBT centers can be grouped under three broad categories: advocacy, services, and education.

Education

It can be argued that virtually all center initiatives are educational in nature; however, some efforts are more explicitly educational than others. Programming is often the most effective and predominant means to educate the campus community outside the classroom on LGBT issues. Campuswide programming efforts should have LGBT and ally concerns embedded within them (e.g., a career-development program on how to write a resume that also addresses LGBT concerns, like the question to include participation in LGBT organizations), yet also specific and with enough depth to address the unique needs of LGBT individuals (e.g., a LGBT-specific career-development workshop *that examines identity management (i.e., if/when/how to come out) in the workplace. Successful programming is often a collaborative process with faculty, student groups, and other campus departments; is frequently student-driven; and has both breadth and depth. Programs with a broad reach enable non-LGBT-identified people to learn and participate in LGBT student life, such as the campuswide Lavender Graduation event that celebrates the accomplishments of LGBT students and provides an easy mechanism for allies to show their support. Programs with depth meet the varying needs of a diverse LGBT student body in different stages of their development (e.g., weekly coming out, transgender, and/or LGBT students of color groups).*

Educational initiatives also take the form of electronic (e.g., an extensive center website) and print resources, a lending library, and the provision of trainings and workshops. Examples of the latter that I have conducted are professional development seminars that help prepare faculty, staff, and administrators to be more effective when working with the LGBT population. Additionally, I have served as a guest lecturer in classes and have offered LGBT-related trainings specifically for resident assistants and orientation leaders.

Services

Among the many services LGBT centers offers are space for a lounge, meetings, studying, and small programs; financial sponsorship for students to attend LGBT conferences (e.g., Creating Change) and LGBT-focused camps (e.g., Camp Pride); scholarships; and the invitation to students to confidentially share their concerns with the director or peer leaders. Many centers also offer internship and service learning opportunities through their office.

Advocacy

Most LGBT center directors, their staff, and advisory boards have a role in LGBT student advocacy. We often provide a vision of LGBT equality and spearhead initiatives to bring greater equity and inclusion to campus policies (e.g., availability of gender neutral restrooms), practices (e.g., including LGBT concerns in official university materials and public addresses), and opportunities (e.g., welcoming options in Greek life). One initiative gaining national momentum is adding optional LGBT-inclusive demographic information on admissions forms to track retention, persistence, and graduation rates of LGBT students. Since sexual orientation and gender identity are attributes that are not visually apparent, many in the LGBT community struggle with feeling invisible and insignificant, and they welcome intentional institutional efforts that recognize their identities and foster their visibility. Therefore, promoting LGBT visibility is an advocacy strategy that leads to a normalization of LGBT issues and promotes a more welcoming campus climate. Visibility is also achieved through queer-friendly symbols in posters, flyers, online information, recruiting materials, and promotional

(Continued)

(Continued)

items such as wristbands, pins, stickers, rainbow flags, T-shirts, and caps. Another effective method to increase LGBT and ally visibility across campus is to award Safe Zone–trained individuals with a certificate that they can display in their living or work spaces.

Visibility is also fostered through the regular use of inclusive language. This means using nonbinary language when discussing gender (e.g., referring to "all" genders rather than "both" genders), using gender-free relational terms (e.g., "partner" or "spouse" rather than "boyfriend"), and gender-neutral pronouns (e.g., "ze," "hir," and "hirs").

—Lisa R. Forest
Bridgewater, Massachusetts

Vignette

University of Southern California LGBT Resource Center

As a national leader in LGBT student services, the LGBT Resource Center at the University of Southern California (USC) sponsors a wide range of innovative social, academic, and advocacy programs and services for the campus community that includes undergraduate and graduate students, faculty, and staff members, USC alumni, and local Los Angeles community members. The center and the LGBT affiliated student organizations have created thought-provoking events and discussions that initiate dialogue about unique student experiences as well as highlight recent campus accomplishments and national LGBT equality achievements.

A few of the USC LGBT Resource Center signature programs and services include the following:

- LGBT Peer Mentoring Program—*a peer-to-peer mentorship program for undergraduate and graduate students to work on their personal, social, academic, career, and lifestyle goals*
- University Rap—*a weekly, peer-facilitated, confidential discussion group for students*
- The Faculty and Staff Allies "Safe Zone" Program—*monthly discussions that educate faculty and staff members about current issues affecting the LGBT community*
- Freshman Advocacy Board—*a first-year emersion program for LGBT and ally first-year students*
- Generation Queer Emerging Leadership Retreat—*a leadership retreat primarily for first-year and transfer students*
- QueerStories Speaker Series—*a series of events that address issues of intersection for LGBT students of color*

- OutReach—*a student organization that provides leadership development, college preparatory skills, and support to local gay–straight alliances in high schools within Los Angeles County*
- Rainbow Floor—*a residential community for LGBT and ally students that sponsors an overnight college experience for prospective students, community building workshops, campuswide events, and volunteer opportunities with LGBT nonprofits*

In 2005, the Advocate College Guide for LGBT Students *named USC among the Top 20 "Best of the Best" LGBT-Friendly Colleges and Universities, and in that same year USC was named a "diversity leader" by the Gender Public Advocacy Coalition (GPAC) due to USC's inclusive nondiscrimination policy that includes sexual orientation, gender identity, and gender expression. This recognition was followed by a "five-star" rating recognition from the LGBT-Friendly Campus Climate Index in 2007. The Los Angeles City Pride Heritage Month Celebration for 2008 also honored the USC LGBT Community with an Achievement Award from the City of Los Angeles.*
For additional information, visit www.usc.edu/lgbt.

—Vincent Vigil, Ed.D., Director

LGBT Resource Center

Division of Student Affairs

Hopefully, there will be a time when all high schools and college settings have an LGBT student center that will support all students. Over the months it took me to write this book, we saw many changes in New York state and the rest of the country. The Dignity for All Students Act was enacted, which means that schools have to have inclusive language in their board policies that include sexual orientation. We also saw the legalization of gay marriage in New York state, which is the sixth and largest state to allow gay marriage. We saw President Obama and U.S. Secretary of Education Arne Duncan talk about safeguarding LGBT students and allowing them equal access to a balanced education. All of these are positive moves forward for the LGBT community.

Unfortunately, there will always be people who do not think the LGBT community deserves equal rights, but I would venture to guess those people have denied many different groups equal rights over the years. It is my hope that they come to grips with their bias and hate because it must take a great deal of energy to spend all of that time hating someone solely based on who they love. In addition, I saw Governor Chris Christie on the news state that he will never allow gay marriage in New Jersey because marriage is between a man and a woman. I truly hope that he understands, as a father, his kids and other kids are watching as he makes such remarks and that only helps to spread the hate. That is the very example of how rampant antigay sentiment is in the country, and comments like that only help perpetuate it.

Educators have a chance every day to make an impact on their students. That impact can be negative or positive. It does not matter if their students are a different religion, race, or sexual orientation. The teachers, counselors, school psychologists, and administrators were hired to protect the rights of all students, and they were hired to make sure that all students receive a quality education. Education can have a powerful influence and can change the lives of all students. It is my hope that you have found some resources that will help you change the climate in your classroom, building, or school district.

Appendix

NASP Position Statement

Lesbian, Gay, Bisexual, Transgender, and Questioning Youth

The National Association of School Psychologists (NASP) supports that all youth have equal opportunities to participate in and benefit from educational and mental health services within schools regardless of sexual orientation, gender identity, or gender expression. Harassment, lack of equal support, and other discriminatory practices toward lesbian, gay, bisexual, transgender, and questioning (LGBTQ) youth violate their rights to receive equal educational opportunities, regardless of whether the discrimination takes the form of direct harassment of individuals or is directed at the entire group through hostile statements or biases. Failure to address discriminatory actions in the school setting compromises student development and achievement. NASP believes that school psychologists are ethically obligated to ensure that all students have an equal opportunity for the development and expression of their personal identity in a school climate that is safe, accepting, and respectful of all persons and free from discrimination, harassment, violence, and abuse. To achieve this goal, education and advocacy must be used to reduce discrimination and harassment against LGBTQ youth by students and staff and promote positive social–emotional and educational development.

When compared to youth who are heterosexual, youth who identify as LGBTQ or those who are gender nonconforming are more likely targeted for harassment and discrimination. For example, when over 7,000 LGBTQ students nationwide were surveyed regarding their school experiences, 84% reported being verbally harassed, 40% reported being physically harassed, and 18% reported being physically assaulted at school within the past year based on actual or perceived sexual orientation (Kosciw, Greytak, Diaz, & Bartkiewicz, 2010). Of the students who reported harassment experiences to school staff, one third said no subsequent school action was taken. Additionally, LGBTQ students were four times more likely than heterosexual students to report skipping at least one day of school in the previous month because they felt unsafe or uncomfortable. While LGBTQ youth appear to experience higher levels of mental health and academic difficulties, school-based social situations like victimization and lack of support are frequently related to these heightened risk levels (Bontempo & D'Augelli., 2002; Goodenow, Szalacha, & Westheimer, 2006). Whereas members of other minority groups likely share their unique identity with family members and a visible community, LGBTQ youth may have few to no opportunities to learn coping strategies related to dealing with anti-LGBTQ sentiments and behaviors from a family support network (Ryan & Futterman, 1998). Additionally, LGBTQ youth are at an increased risk for emotional and physical rejection by their families and may become homeless as a result of disclosing their sexual orientation or gender identity (Rivers & D'Augelli, 2001). Concealing one's LGBTQ identity may increase a youth's risk for anxiety, depression, hostility, demoralization, guilt, shame, social avoidance, isolation, and impaired relationships (Pachankis, 2007).

CREATING SAFE SCHOOLS FOR LGBTQ YOUTH

Individual and systems-level advocacy, education, and specific intervention efforts are needed to create safe and supportive schools for LGBTQ youth. These should include, but not be limited to, the following strategies.

Establish and enforce comprehensive nondiscrimination and anti-bullying policies that include LGBTQ issues. Many schools already have nondiscrimination policies, but these may not include reference to sexual orientation, gender identity, or gender expression. Explicitly including these characteristics in policy statements gives legitimacy to LGBTQ concerns and keeps schools accountable for enforcing nondiscrimination and antibullying standards. Explicit policies also support staff who may fear repercussions for openly intervening and advocating for LGBTQ youth.

Educate students and staff. NASP supports educating students and staff about LGBTQ youth and their needs through professional development about the range of normal human diversity that includes sexual orientation, gender identity, and gender expression. Professional development training can lead to immediate and maintained improvements in students' and educators' motivation to interrupt harassing remarks and increased awareness of LGBTQ issues and resources (Greytak & Kosciw, 2010). NASP also supports the provision of information and training about relevant research, the risks experienced by these youth, effective strategies for addressing harassment and discrimination directed toward any student, and improving the school climate (e.g., inservices, staff development, policy development, research briefs, and program implementation). In addition, creating an educational context that includes the broad array of human diversity can help demystify sexual orientation and gender identity, along with promoting a positive self-concept for LGBTQ youth. This can include infusing issues pertaining to sexual orientation and gender identity into the curriculum, which may decrease feelings of isolation and promote a more positive self-concept. Curricula may include presenting theories about the development of sexual orientation or gender identity in a science class; reading works of famous gay, lesbian, bisexual, or transgender authors in a literature class; discussing the LGBTQ rights movement in historical context with other civil rights movements in a social studies class; or including LGBTQ demographic statistics in math exercises. In addition, including LGBTQ issues in health education can increase decision-making skills for all youth by preparing them to make positive choices and reducing unsafe behavior.

Intervene directly with perpetrators. As with any instance of school violence, harassment and discrimination against LGBTQ youth, or any gender nonconforming youth, should be addressed both through applying consequences and educating the perpetrator. Education should be provided to the perpetrator to help prevent future aggression. Interventions should emphasize that discrimination and harassment must be addressed regardless of the status of the perpetrator. Youth, teachers, support staff, and administrators must be educated to make policies effective.

Provide intervention and support for those students targeted for harassment and intimidation and those exploring their sexuality or gender identity. Up to one fourth of adolescents may question their sexual orientation or gender identity (Hollander, 2000). School personnel should make no assumptions about youth who may be questioning, but provide opportunities for students to develop healthy identities. In addition to sexual orientation, gender identity, and gender expression, other diversity characteristics (e.g., gender, ethnicity, socioeconomic status) may add additional challenges or serve as strengths toward positive mental health and academic development and should be considered. Counseling and other supports should be made available for students who have been targets of harassment, for those who are questioning their sexual orientation or gender identity, for those who are perceived as LGBTQ by peers or others, and for those who may become targets of harassment in the future by disclosing their status as LGBTQ (e.g., Gay-Straight Alliance). Interventions should focus on strategies that allow students to experience safety and respect in the school environment, including empowerment of students to address harassment of students who are LGBTQ.

Promote societal and familial attitudes and behaviors that affirm the dignity and rights within educational environments of LGBTQ youth. Schools should promote awareness, acceptance, and accommodation of LGBTQ students and their needs in fair ways. Schools can promote attitudes that affirm the dignity and rights of LGBTQ youth by becoming aware of and eliminating biases from their own practice. They can model nondiscriminatory practice by providing services to all students regardless of sexual orientation, gender identity/expression, or other minority status. School psychologists can promote and model affirming attitudes, use language that is nondiscriminatory and inclusive, and educate students and staff. Moreover, schools can function as powerful agents of change when they actively address slurs and openly confront discrimination, and they can address the actions or statements of other school staff or administrators who neglect the needs of LGBTQ youth or who actively discriminate against them. School psychologists can provide information, expert opinions, and evidence-based strategies to ensure that effective policies and practices are adopted and enforced, increasing the acceptance and tolerance of differences in the school environment by supporting development of student groups that promote understanding and acceptance of human diversity. Gay-straight alliances (GSAs) have a positive impact on school climate (Kosciw, Diaz, Greytak, & Bartkiewicz, 2010) and should be supported by school psychologists. Students who reported having GSAs in their schools were less likely to feel unsafe, less likely to miss school, and were more likely to feel that they belonged at their school than students in school with no such clubs (Kosciw et al.). Schools should also be informed about programs in the community that facilitate and support healthy development of LGBTQ youth and support their families, and be prepared to advise parents, school personnel, and youth about these resources.

Recognize strengths and resilience. While much of the research has focused on negative factors impacting the development of LGBTQ youth, there are strengths as well. Savin-Williams (2009) posits a developmental trajectory that can impact a student positively or negatively with regard to psychosocial and educational domains. Further review of the research indicates that LGBTQ youth are capable of developing methods to keep themselves safe and find support from their environment. School psychologists should work to identify and build strengths and resilience in LGBTQ youth.

ROLE OF THE SCHOOL PSYCHOLOGIST

School psychologists can function as role models of ethical practice and inform staff and students that they are available to all students regardless of sexual orientation or gender identity. School psychologists can address issues of sexual orientation and gender identity in inservice training with teachers and programming for parents, actively counter discriminatory practices, and utilize NASP and other resources to advocate for LGBTQ youth. On an individual level, in counseling sessions, school psychologists can be mindful that sexual orientation, gender identity, and gender expression encompass a broad spectrum, and that many students question their sexual orientation and gender identity or are gender nonconforming. School psychologists are also in a position to educate students about a number of issues related to high risk behaviors that are especially frequent among gay, lesbian, bisexual, transgender, and questioning youth, creating a more inclusive and healthier environment for both the school population in general and LGBTQ youth in particular.

SUMMARY

NASP recognizes that students who identify as LGBTQ, or those who are gender nonconforming, may be at risk for experiencing harassment and discrimination, as well as risk factors for social, emotional, and academic problems related to psychosocial stressors (Bontempo & D'Augelli, 2002; D'Augelli, 2006; Ryan & Futterman 1998). A successful program to address these issues educates both those who discriminate and those who are discriminated against because of sexual orientation, gender identity, or gender nonconformity. School psychologists can participate in education and advocacy on a number of levels by promoting nondiscrimination policies; conducting schoolwide inservice training; actively addressing discrimination and neglect of student needs; sharing information about human diversity and evidence-based practices to address student needs; and modeling ethical practice through accepting and affirming attitudes, language, and behaviors in daily interactions with all students and staff. In addition, school psychologists can provide intervention to individual students. Any program designed to address the needs of LGBTQ youth should also include efforts to educate and support parents and the community through collecting information about services and establishing involvement with other organizations committed to equal opportunity for education and mental health services for all youth. Schools can only be truly safe when every student, regardless of sexual orientation, gender identity, and gender expression, is assured of access to an education without fear of harassment, discrimination, or violence.

REFERENCES

Bontempo, D., & D'Augelli, A. (2002). Effects of at-school victimization and sexual orientation on lesbian, gay, or bisexual youths' health risk behavior. *Journal of Adolescent Health, 30*, 364–374.

D'Augelli, A. (2006). Developmental and contextual factors and mental health among lesbian, gay, and bisexual youths. In A. Omoto & H. Kurtzman (Eds.), *Sexual orientation and mental health: Examining identity and development in lesbian, gay and bisexual people* (pp. 37–53). Washington, DC: American Psychological Association.

Goodenow, C., Szalacha, L., & Westheimer, K. (2006). School support groups, other school factors, and the safety of sexual minority adolescents. *Psychology in the Schools, 43,* 573–589. doi: 10.1002/pits.20173

Greytak, E. A., & Kosciw, J. G. (2010). Year one evaluation of the New York City Department of Education *Respect for All* training program. New York, NY: GLSEN.

Hollander, G. (2000). Questioning youth: Challenges to working with youths forming identities. *School Psychology Review, 29,* 173–179.

Kosciw, J. G., Greytak, E. A., Diaz, E. M., & Bartkiewicz, M. J. (2010). *The 2009 National School Climate Survey: The experiences of lesbian, gay, bisexual, and transgender youth in our nation's school.* New York, NY: GLSEN.

Pachankis, J. E. (2007). The psychological implications of concealing a stigma: A cognitive-affective behavioral model. *Psychological Bulletin, 133,* 328–345. doi:10.1037/0033-.2909.133.2.328

Rivers, I., & D'Augelli, A. (2001). The victimization of lesbian, gay, and bisexual youths. In A. D'Augelli & C. Patterson (Eds.), *Lesbian, gay and bisexual identities and youth: Psychological perspectives* (pp. 199–223). New York, NY: Oxford University Press.

Ryan, C., & Futterman, D. (1998). *Lesbian and gay youth: Care and counseling.* New York, NY: Columbia University Press.

Savin-Williams, R. C. (2009). How many gays are there? It depends. In D. A. Hope (Ed.), *Contemporary perspectives on lesbian, gay, and bisexual identities* (pp. 5–41). New York, NY: Springer.

References

Agirdag, O., & Van Houtte, M. (2011). A tale of two cities: Bridging families and schools. *Educational Leadership, 68*(8), 42–46.

Anderson, D. A. (1995). Lesbian and gay adolescents: Social and developmental considerations. In G. Unks (Ed.), *The gay teen: Educational practice and theory for lesbian, gay, and bisexual adolescents* (pp. 17–28). New York, NY: Routledge.

Biegel, S. (2011). Teachable moments. *The Advocate, 1048*, 20–21.

Bielaczyc, M. S. (2001). *Building communities, understanding complexities: How does an independent school head encourage parents and trustees to support the inclusion of gay and lesbian issues at an independent school?* New York, NY: GLSEN.

Blumenfeld, W. J. (2010). *The media, suicide, and homophobia.* Retrieved from http://sometimesdaveywins.blogspot.com.

Burrow-Sanchez, J. J., & Lopez, A. L. (2009). Identifying substance abuse issues in high schools: A national survey of high school counselors. *Journal of Counseling & Development, 87*(1), 72–79.

Cha, S. (2003). *The influence of school administrators' transfer—Enhancing supervisory practices in teachers' transfer of learning.* Madison: University of Wisconsin–Madison.

Cochrane, D. (2004). Christian opposition to homosexuality. In J. McNinch & M. Cronin (Eds.), *I could not speak my heart: Education and social justice for gay and lesbian youth* (pp. 163–171). Saskatchewan, Canada: University of Regina.

deMarrais, K. B., & LeCompte, M. D. (1999). *The way schools work: A sociological analysis of education.* Reading, MA: Longman.

DeWitt, P. (2011). *A qualitative case study: How school administrators safeguard sexually diverse students.* Doctoral dissertation, Albany, NY: Sage College.

DeWitt, P. (2011). The effects of bullying on GLBT Students. *ASCD Express,* 6.13. Retrieved from http://www.ascd.org/ascd-express/vol6/613-dewitt.aspx.

DeWitt, P. (2011, May). Dignity for all. *Vanguard Magazine,* 11–15.

Duncan, A. (2011). *Dear colleague letter.* Washington, DC: U.S. Department of Education.

Edwards, A. T. (1997). Let's stop ignoring our gay and lesbian youth. *Educational Leadership, 54*(7), 68–70.

Flores, G. (2009). *Teachers' attitudes in implementing gay-themed literature as part of a balanced multi-cultural education curriculum.* Phoenix, AZ: University of Phoenix.

Foderaro, L. W. (2010, September 29). Private moment made public, then a fatal jump. *New York Times.* Retrieved from http://www.nytimes.com/2010/09/30/nyregion/30suicide.html.

Friend, R. (1998). *Invisible children in the society and the schools.* London: Lawrence Erlbaum.

Fullen, M. (2001). *Leading in a culture of change.* San Francisco, CA: Jossey-Bass.

Gates, G. J. (2006). *Same-sex couples and the gay, lesbian, bisexual population: New estimates from the American Community Survey.* Los Angeles, CA: The Williams Institute, UCLA School of Law.

Gay Straight Alliance (n.d.). *Gay–straight alliance.* Retrieved October 3, 2009, from http://www.gaystraightalliance.org

GLSEN. (2007). *The GLSEN jump start guide: Building and activating your GSA or similar student club.* New York, NY: Author.

GLSEN. (2008). *The principal's perspective: School safety, bullying, and harrassment.* New York, NY: Author.

GLSEN. (2009). *2009 National School Climate Survey: The experiences of lesbian, gay, bisexual and transgender youth in our nation's schools.* New York, NY: Author.

GLSEN. (2010). *Dealing with legal matters surrounding students' sexual orientation and gender identity.* New York, NY: Author.

Gordon, L. (1995). What do we say when we hear the word 'faggot'? In L. Delpit, H. L. Gates, H. Kohl, & H. Zinn (Eds.), *Rethinking schools* (pp. 40–44). New York, NY: New York Press.

Harbeck, K. M. (1995). Invisible no more: Addressing the needs of lesbian, gay, and bisexual youth and their advocates. In G. Unks (Ed.), *The gay teen: Educational practice and theory for lesbian, gay, and bisexual adolescents* (pp. 125–133). New York, NY: Routledge.

Hirsch, A. J. (2007). *Future teachers' attitudes and anticipated behaviors toward sexual minority youth.* Ann Arbor, MI: Michigan State University.

Housman, A. E. (1936). *XXXI* (First ed.). Bedford Square, London: Jonathan Cape.

Horowitz, A., & Itzkowitz, M. (2011). LGBTQ youth in American schools: Moving to the middle. *Middle School Journal, 42*(5), 32–38.

Kosciw, J. G. (2007). *2007 National School Climate Survey: Key findings on the experiences of lesbian, gay, bisexual and transgendered youth in our nation's schools.* New York, NY: GLSEN.

Lipkin, A. (1995). The case for a gay and lesbian curriculum. In G. Unks (Ed.), *The gay teen: Educational practice and theory for lesbian, gay, and bisexual adolescents* (pp. 31–52). New York, NY: Routledge.

Lugg, C. A., & Shoho, A. R. (2006). Dare public school administrators build a new social order? *Journal of Educational Administration, 44*(3), 196–208.

Marinoble, R. M. (1998). Counseling and supporting our gay students. *The Education Digest, 46,* 54–59.

McLaren, P. (1995). Moral panic, schooling, and the politics of resistance. In G. Unks (Ed.), *The gay teen: Educational practice and theory for lesbian, gay, and bisexual adolescents* (pp. 105–123). New York, NY: Routledge.

McNinch, J., & Cronin, M. (2004). *I could not speak my heart: Education and social justice for gay and lesbian youth.* Canadian Plains Research Center, University of Regina: Regina, SK.

O'Conor, A. (1995). Breaking the silence: Writing about gay, lesbian, and bisexual teenagers. In G. Unks, *The gay teen: Educational practice and theory for lesbian, gay, and bisexual adolescents* (pp. 13–15). New York, NY: Routledge.

Rankin, S., Weber, G., Blumenfeld, W., & Frazer, S. (2010). "2010 State of Higher Education for Lesbian, Gay, Bisexual, and Transgender People." *Campus Pride,* Charlotte, NC.

Robelen, E. W. (2011). California may mandate inclusion of gay history in curricula. *Education Week, 30*(29), 10.

Rofes, E. (1995). Making our schools safe for sissies. In G. Unks (Ed.), *The gay teen: Educational practice and theory for lesbian, gay, and bisexual adolescents* (pp. 79–84). New York, NY: Routledge.

Roper, L. D. (2005). The role of senior student affaris officers in supporting LGBT students: Exploring the landscape of one's life. *New Directions for Student Services, 111,* 81–88.

Ross, B., Schwartz, R., Mosk, M., & Chuchmach, M. (Writers). (2011, July 11). Pray the gay away. In *Nightline.* New York, NY: ABC.

Russell, S. T. (2011, March 30). Changing policy to end anti-gay bullying. *Education Week.* Retrieved from http://www.edweek.org/ew/articles/2011/03/30/26russell.h30.html.

Russell, S. T., Muraco, A., Subramaniam, A., & Laub, C. (2009, January 10). Youth empowerment and high school gay–straight alliances. *Journal of Youth Adolescence, 38*(7), 891–903.

Ryan, C. (2009). *Supportive families, healthy children helping families with lesbian, gay, bisexual & transgender children.* San Francisco, CA: San Francisco State University.

Sadowski, M. (2010). Beyond gay–straight alliances. *Education Digest,* *76*(1), 12–16.

Savage, T. A., & Harley, D. (2009). A place at the blackboard: LGBTIQ. *Multicultural Education, 16,* 2–9.

Savage, D., & Miller, T. (2011). *It gets better. Coming out, overcoming bullying, and creating a life worth living.* New York, NY: Dutton.

Schneck, K. M. (2008). *That's so gay! Deconstructing the word gay and its place in the daily parlance of high school students.* New York, NY: Fordham University.

Sears, J. T. (1991). Helping students understand and accept sexual diversity. *The Education Digetst, 57*(4), 53–55.

Senge, P. M., Cambron McCabe, N. H., Lucas, T., Kleiner, A., Dutton, J., & Smith, B. (2000). Schools that learn: A fifth discipline fieldbook for educators, parents, and everyone who cares about education. Doubleday: New York, NY.

Shah, N. (2011). Duncan warns schools on banning gay–straight clubs. *Education Week.* Retrieved from http://www.edweek.org/ew/articles/2 011/06/14/36gaystraight.h30.html.

Stolberg, S. (2011, July 17). For Bachmann, gay rights stand reflects mix of issues and faith. *New York Times.* Retrieved from http://www.nytimes. com/2011/07/17/us/politics/17bachmann.html?pagewanted=all.

Szalacha, L. (2001). *The sexual diversity climate of Massachusetts' secondary schools and the success of the safe schools program for gay and lesbian students.* Boston, MA: Harvard University.

Szalacha, L. (2003). Safer sexual diversity climates: Lessons learned from an evaluation of the Massachusetts Safe Schools Program for gay and lesbian students. *American Journal of Education, 110,* 58–88.

Thiede, H., Valleroy, L. A., MacKellar, D. A., Celentano, D. D., Ford, W. L., Hagan, H., Koblin, B. A., … Torian, L. V. (2003). Regional patterns and correlates of substance use among young men who have sex with men in 7 US urban areas. *American Journal of Public Health, 93,* 11, 1915–1921.

Trachtenberg, R., & Bachtell, T. (2005). *When I knew.* New York, NY: HarperCollins Publishers.

Unks, G. (1995). *The gay teen: Educational practice and theory for lesbian, gay, and bisexual adolescents.* New York, NY: Routledge.

Weiler, E. (2003). Making school safe for sexual minority students. *Principal Leadership Magazine, 4*(4). Retrieved from http://www. nasponline.org/resources/principals/nassp_glbqt.aspx.

Whelan, D. L. (2009). A dirty little secret. *School Library Journal, 55*(2), 26–30.

Whitaker, T. (2003). *What great principals do differently.* Columbus, OH: Eye on Education.

Index

CORWIN
A SAGE Company

The Corwin logo—a raven striding across an open book—represents the union of courage and learning. Corwin is committed to improving education for all learners by publishing books and other professional development resources for those serving the field of PreK–12 education. By providing practical, hands-on materials, Corwin continues to carry out the promise of its motto: **"Helping Educators Do Their Work Better."**

NATIONAL ASSOCIATION OF SCHOOL PSYCHOLOGISTS

The National Association of School Psychologists represents school psychology and supports school psychologists to enhance the learning and mental health of all children and youth.